Jeanne Argent
**Imaginative
Leatherwork**

Jeanne Argent
Imaginative Leatherwork

David & Charles

Newton Abbot   London   Vancouver

0 7153 6654 8

Set in 11 on 13 Baskerville by Wordsworth Typesetting, London and
printed in Great Britain by Redwood Burn Ltd, Trowbridge and Esher for
David & Charles (Holdings) Limited South Devon House Newton Abbot Devon.

Published in Canada by Douglas David & Charles Limited 3645
McKechnie Drive West Vancouver BC

Contents

Introduction

The purpose of this book is to introduce an interesting and rewarding material to those who have not worked with leather before, but who are perhaps familiar with other crafts and generally 'good with their hands'.

Recently, there has been a revival of interest in a variety of crafts. Evening classes for woodwork, pottery, jewellery, leatherwork and dressmaking have become filled with people who are tired of mass-produced goods and are looking for something to work at in their spare time which is not only satisfying, but has an end product which is their own work.

For a few years now leatherwork has been considered by some to be rather a dowdy craft consisting mainly of making small purses and bags which are thonged or laced together round the edges in 'peasant-style'. Part of the reason for this misapprehension has been the lack of general literature on the subject and the rarity of patterns, apart from glove patterns, which are designed especially for the amateur leatherworker. I hope that, to some extent, the following pages will rectify this.

Of all crafts, leatherwork is one of the oldest. It began when men first clothed themselves in the skins of the animals they killed for food. Curing and tanning techniques have been gradually improved down the ages and special tools evolved for shaping and joining this material. Many interesting leather items have been found in tombs of the Ancient Egyptians.

In medieval times leather and wood were the most plentiful materials available and so leather was used for drinking vessels and many other household items today produced in china and glass. All these items were made by hand by the leatherworker, who was as commonplace a sight as the local village blacksmith or carpenter.

These days, with so many things being made from pre-fabricated, mass-produced materials, leather is becoming a luxury material. Manufacturers of most plastic-coated fabrics try to imitate the appearance of leather instead of enhancing the good qualities of their own particular material to produce something that is clearly synthetic, but attractive in its own right. So the chances are that when you make your first item from leather one of your friends will poke it and say 'It's not real leather, though, is it?'.

No matter how much it is imitated, however, there is always a great difference between the real thing and any reproduction. Real leather is porous; it breathes and is therefore ideal for making warm and healthy clothing. It smells nice; it has a texture and feels good; and these days, with improved dyeing techniques, glorious colours can be achieved. It does not fray or tear easily and can be stuck, sewn, riveted or laced together. It can be laminated and carved or moulded into different shapes when dampened, or it can be patterned and tooled, fringed or trimmed with metal studs. What more could you wish from a natural material?

One of the most satisfying things about working with leather is its infinite variety. It can be as stiff and hard as a piece of wood or as soft and supple as fine silk; in between these two extremes you have all the leathers suitable for clothing, luggage, harness, furniture and industrial purposes. The colours available nowadays cover the whole spectrum, whilst some leathers are given special finishes to make them either waterproof, very shiny, or hand-washable.

Because of this variety, the book has been divided into two distinct sections. Each part is followed by a selection of designs, with scaled patterns and instructions for making things using the methods already described.

Part 1 deals with the craft of leatherwork and explains the various tools and techniques used to make wallets, bags, folios, etc.

Part 2 is devoted to the dressmaking side of working with leather and describes how to adapt patterns and standard dressmaking procedures to suit leather and suede.

Leather – the Material

Most of the leather that is available these days comes from the skins of the animals we kill for food: cows, sheep, goats and pigs. These skins and hides are produced in many parts of the world; some are tanned in the country where they are killed whilst others are treated for preservation before being shipped to other countries for processing into leather. Preservation of some sort is necessary because skins and hides in their natural state will soon putrefy and decompose. The usual method is to pack them into boxes and barrels with layers of salt.

When they reach their destination the first stage of the process is the cleaning away of all traces of salt. Then, together with local, unpreserved skins, they are prepared for tanning. First of all the hair or wool is thoroughly removed, together with all traces of sweat glands, hair follicles and dead cells. This is achieved by scraping after immersing them in a solution of lime which loosens these unwanted parts. The flesh side is then prepared by cutting away unwanted tissue from the inside of the skin. In days gone by, the operations of scraping and 'fleshing' were carried out by hand by skilled workers, but machines are now used.

Very often a skin or hide is too thick for the purpose for which it is finally intended, so it has to be shaved or split.

Splitting means cutting the hide before tanning into two or more layers, using a highly accurate band knife machine. In the olden times the only way of making a skin or hide thinner was to shave it by hand on the flesh side with a special tool known as the currier's knife. This job needed great skill, like most of the old leather trades. The thin pieces shaved off were virtually useless. Today machine splitting means that each separate layer can be used, although the top or grain layer is always the best quality because of its grain. Some skins are still shaved, but by machine instead of by hand, and at a later stage, after tanning, to make the skin an even thickness all over.

When all the dirt, fat, unwanted tissue, hair, traces of lime, etc have been removed, the skins and hides are ready to be made into leather by one of the three main tanning processes.

VEGETABLE TANNING

This is the original process from which the word tanning is derived, the tannin from different barks being used to process the skins into leather. Skins and hides were layered in pits with the bark and water and left to soak. The pits were emptied every few months and relayered with fresh bark to make different strengths of infusion, the whole process taking up to eighteen months. Pits or vats are still used for some hides, but tannic acid is obtained nowadays from various plants instead of using bark in its raw state. The highest quality hides may still spend several months in the pits, in gradually strengthening tanning solutions. Smaller skins can be processed in a matter of days in huge revolving drums filled with the tanning solution. The finished colour of vegetable tanned leathers ranges from pale cream to a deep reddish-brown.

CHROME OR MINERAL TANNING

Alum was the original mineral used for this, together with salt, to produce a stiff, pure white leather, examples of which have been found dating back to Ancient Egypt. In the nineteenth century, chromium salts were first used to produce a leather which was highly resistant to water. This was a major development in the tanning industry and today most leather used for footwear and clothing is chrome tanned. The process is more or less the same as for vegetable tanning, large hides being soaked in pits or vats, and smaller skins in revolving drums. After chrome tanning the colour of the leather is a pale, bluish green.

OIL TANNING OR 'CHAMOISING'

Prehistoric man treated his skins by working animal fats into them to make them soft and supple; this did not produce a true leather, it merely prolonged the life of the skin. Nowadays, skins are impregnated with fish oils which are then allowed to oxidise in the air. This produces a proper leather by chemical action. The skins are squeezed very dry, then pounded with heavy wooden hammers and sprinkled with the fish oil. This process is repeated several times; then the skins are hung in a drying room whilst the oxidisation takes place and finally washed to remove any excess oil. Skins produced in this way are very soft and supple. Chamois leather is probably the best known, being made from sheep skin from which the grain layer has been removed by splitting. The grain split which has been removed is probably used for skiver or lining.

FINISHING

The tanned leathers are finished in a wide variety of ways depending on what they are finally intended for. Most leathers are dressed with oils or fats of some sort to give them durability, and this is usually impregnated in heated revolving drums. Flexibility is often improved by pulling the leather over specially shaped blunt blades in different directions to stretch it. This is called staking because originally it was done over a stake driven into the ground. Some leathers are made harder and firmer in texture by compressing them through heavy rollers. This used to be done in the old days by hammering them evenly all over. Others are treated by hand with tallow and cod oil to make them strong and flexible. This is called currying, and leathers treated in this way are used for harness, upholstery and industrial purposes.

The surface of leather is also finished by many different methods to produce widely differing textures. Some skins and hides have their grain surface buffed or sanded to remove scars and blemishes; others are finished by buffing on the flesh side to make suede. Colour is applied in several different ways – by dyeing in a dye-bath, by spraying, or, for high quality leathers, by staining by hand. Surfaces are made smooth and shiny or textured either by hand or by machine.

Many high quality hides and skins are dyed or stained and finished in a way which allows all the natural grain of the leather, imperfections and all, to show through. Some of these leathers are 'boarded', that is folded then rolled all over either by hand or by machine to give a softly creased effect over the entire surface. Others are left smooth and uncreased. Some leathers are given a pig-mented or lacquered finish which completely covers up the grain surface and makes it quite plain and featureless, whilst others are buffed and re-printed with another type of grain. An example of this is pig-grained sheep, where the smooth surface of the sheepskin is given an all-over pattern to simulate pigskin with its characteristic texture of three little holes in triangular formation. Grain patterns like this are usually produced by passing the leather through engraved, heated rollers. Other finishes include plating or glazing, using special metal or glass tools to give a smooth, shiny surface; patent leather, which has a very highly polished surface, is given many coats of daubs, varnishes and lacquers; suede is produced by buffing and fluffing the flesh side to raise a nap of small fibres. Velvet calf is also produced in this way, but the grain side is buffed instead of the flesh side.

Most oil-tanned leather is not given any sophisticated finishing process; sometimes it is dyed, particularly the best quality skins which are used for clothing and gloves. Much of it is left in a natural undyed state and used for wash leathers and industrial purposes.

Part 1
The Craft
of Leatherwork

So many things are made by machine these days that some people have the idea that hand-made items must necessarily be inferior in appearance or construction to machine-made ones. Quite the reverse is true. Although the machine scores perhaps on precision and accuracy, it cannot have any feeling for the materials it works with and therefore cannot take the extra care and pride in the work which, after all, is what craftsmanship in any material is all about.

In order to create beautiful things from any material you must feel enthusiastic about the material itself. It is this enthusiasm which enables you to overcome the problems and master the various techniques necessary to practise the craft.

Leather is a material which appeals to a great many people. As well as its obvious good looks, it is pleasant to handle; its texture is interesting and it has a very distinctive and intriguing smell. Of all natural materials, it is perhaps the most versatile, as well as being one of the most convenient to work with at home.

A great deal of space is not required for leatherwork – most of the different skills can be practised on the kitchen table. Little mess is involved; there are no sawdust, noisy machinery, nasty-smelling materials or dangerous chemicals to deal with, and most of the tools and equipment needed can be kept in a shoe-box or small drawer.

Once you have bought your tools expenses are limited to the leather itself, thread, adhesives and linings. Good tools will last you a lifetime, provided you look after them properly, keep them well sharpened and free from rust or dirt. Although the leather itself is sometimes quite expensive to buy, when you look around at the price of most leather goods in the shops you will see that once you have mastered the basic techniques you will be able to make similar goods for less than half the price. Gifts in leather are also very acceptable to most people.

If you have never made anything from leather before, it is best to get the feel of the material by making something very simple first of all. Practice is the only way to become skilled, so buy an inexpensive skin and make a simple sheath for the carving knife, or a watch strap, or a small purse, and get the feel of the tools by practising cutting and sewing. When you have really mastered this, you can then make something larger and more complicated with a more expensive piece of leather. While it is a great shame to use good leather for practising, it is equally sad to spend a great deal of time and skill in making something from an inferior skin, since the finished work will never have that quality look.

All the patterns shown in Part One of this book can be assembled using the tools and the techniques described on the next few pages. I have kept all the patterns as simple as possible, but once you have made one or two of them you will probably want to design something for yourself.

If you look around at leather goods on display in shops, you will soon be able to ascertain how they are cut and joined. Inspiration can be found for many items and you can design and make bags, cases, etc which are planned around the items they are intended to hold. For example, your first project in designing might be to group all the items you usually try to jam into your wallet into similar sizes and shapes, and then design a new wallet tailored to fit them. The basic stages for the wallet on p65 can be followed, but to your new measurements.

All sorts of useful and decorative ideas can be noted and stored away for some future project. A sketchbook is useful, or a scrapbook, so that you can clip out interesting pictures from magazines and catalogues and paste them into it. Try not to copy these things exactly, but adapt the styles and details to suit your own purposes and to produce a design which is your own rather than a copy of someone else's.

When you are looking for ideas, pay special attention to the way in which some buckles, studs and other fastenings are used so that they are decorative as well as functional. Part of a good design is the choice of suitable fastenings and handles to suit the shape and size of the item. Not only must these fastenings etc be sufficiently durable, they must also complement the item they are attached to for a well-balanced design.

There are some aspects of leatherwork which this introduction inevitably cannot cover. But once you have acquired the basic techniques, you can explore other methods and go on to develop your own particular style of leatherwork.

Leatherwork Tools

Good tools are an essential part of any craft, and in the long run, good quality, and perhaps rather more expensive tools will work out much better value than cheaper ones made from inferior materials and not so well designed. Owing to the cost involved, it is wise to take good care of all your tools and to protect them carefully from misuse or damage.

Knives and other edge tools should always be kept sharp and clean; the blades should be protected from contact with metal objects and other things which could dull or chip them. Very often simple knife sheaths can be assembled from offcuts of leather, and making these is good practice in cutting and sewing.

The oilstone used to sharpen your tools should always be wiped clean after use, and anything to do with oil should be kept well away from the surface on which the leather is worked. Lids must be replaced firmly on stain and adhesive jars and tubes as soon as they are finished with, and the brushes cleaned immediately to prevent them hardening and becoming useless.

Take care to see that cutting boards are always clean. A lot of damage can be done if trimmings from some other job are left on the board to get under the knife. Always

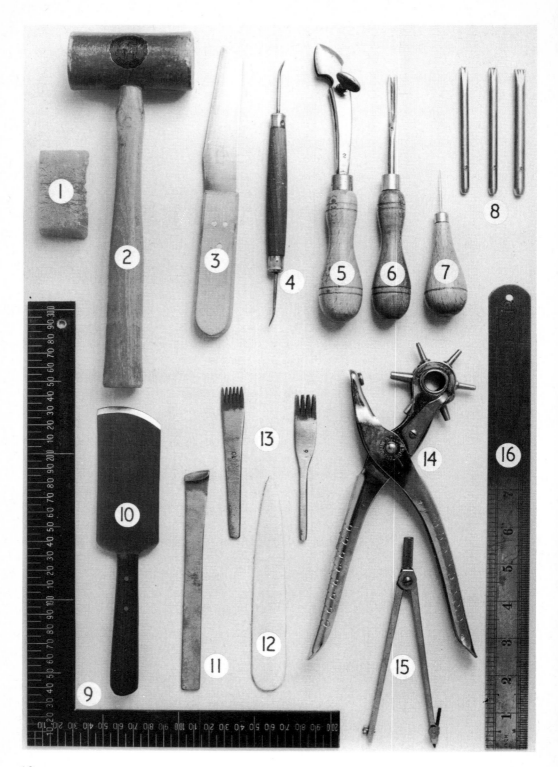

clear away the offcuts as soon as they are made. I usually sort mine out as I go along, the largish pieces go into a box for small jobs and patchwork, and the really small bits go straight into the wastepaper bin.

When glueing or pasting, it is a good idea to have several layers of paper on the bench. The top layer can then be removed when it gets grubby and gummed up and the next sheet used.

Linen thread has a nasty habit of unwinding itself in a drawer full of tools and tangling everything together, so keep your reels of thread in boxes away from tools and tape the ends down with Sellotape after use.

Always keep a tidy work surface, and lay pieces of leather out flat when they are not being worked on. Don't lay tools on the cut out pieces, because the weight of the tool can damage the leather.

SOME TOOLS YOU WILL NEED

Measuring

A good steel ruler is essential both for measuring and for using as a straight edge when cutting out. A 2ft long one is best, especially for cutting out larger shapes, but a smaller one will do if this is not easily obtainable.

A set-square is also very necessary for obtaining accurate right-angled corners and lines, and you will find the transparent celluloid ones useful for marking out. These should never be used as a cutting guide, however, since they easily become cut and inaccurate. A steel set-square is recommended for cutting out.

A selection of leatherwork tools: 1, beeswax; 2, raw-hide mallet; 3, cutting-out knife; 4, modelling tool or fid; 5, adjustable screw creaser; 6, edge shave; 7, diamond awl; 8, selection of decorative modelling punches; 9, set-square; 10, skiving knife; 11, race; 12, bone folder; 13, stitch markers or pricking irons; 14, six-way hole punch; 15, compass; 16, steel ruler

A protractor is invaluable for making templates for patchwork shapes and for working out oblique angles for corners. Again, the transparent celluloid type is most useful because markings can be clearly seen through it.

For marking out circles of different sizes, and for measuring distances between points, a pair of dividers or compasses are necessary. You can use the type supplied with school geometry sets, but better still is the kind which can be set by means of a screw. These are less likely to move out of position halfway round a circle.

Knives and Sharpeners

Sharp knives are essential to every cutting operation and therefore you should always buy the best you can afford and keep them really well sharpened.

19

To begin with, you will need two basic types – the cutting knife for cutting out shapes from the leather, and the skiving knife, for paring off unwanted thickness. The cutting knife is sometimes also called the shoemaker's knife and is available from most good craft shops. The skiving knife looks a bit like a short chisel with a slanted, rounded blade. This is also bevelled on one side like a chisel. It is supplied in either left- or right-handed versions, and when held in the correct hand the bevelled side should be facing upwards and the leading edge of the blade facing inwards, ie right for a right-handed person and left for a left-handed person.

Craft knives with replaceable blades are also useful tools to have, particularly those which have interchangeable curved, straight and oblique blades. A word of warning – if you use them a lot on leather, the blades could work out quite costly, since they tend to dull very quickly. It is an excellent idea to use an old craft knife for cutting out cardboard and paper patterns, and reserve the good sharp blades for the leather.

Your cutting or shoemaker's knife will probably be bought with a dull edge, and will need to be sharpened before use. For this you will need an oilstone, some oil and an emery board which you can make yourself. The best type of oilstone is the double-sided one which is coarser on one side than the other. Use the coarse side first with a drop or two of sewing-machine oil and grind the edge of the blade on this. Then wipe this side of the stone and use the fine side in the same way. When you are satisfied with the sharpness of your blade, it should be polished on the emery board and then stropped to give it a really keen edge.

To make your own emery and strop board, take a piece of wood about 15in long, 2in wide and ½in thick and shape one end into a handle as shown in the diagram. To one side of this, glue a strip of fine emery cloth, and to the other side, a piece of hide with the flesh side facing outwards. Rub the hide with a piece of beeswax or tallow, then when you have ground your knife on the stone, polish it several times on the emery side of the board, always with the back of the knife leading, never the blade. If you are using the knife for thick and heavy leathers, there is no need to strop it, but for fine leather or chamois a really keen edge is called for. Sprinkle a little fine emery

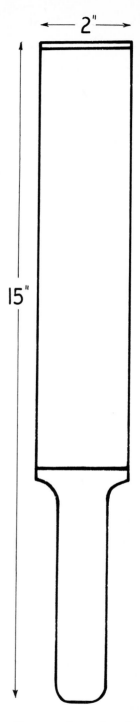

Emery and stropboard

powder on to the hide and run the knife over it several times, with the back of the knife leading and changing direction at each end of the board. When turning the knife over for the return, turn it so that the blade faces away from the board each time. This may seem a little awkward at first, but you will soon get used to it, and will not risk damaging the blade by bumping it on the board.

Cutting Boards

For cutting out shapes on a flat surface, the best type of board is made from pieces of softwood glued together with the end-grain facing upwards. When the knife cuts down into this, the blade opens up the grain of the wood which closes when the knife has passed. This means that, provided you keep the knife at right angles to the surface of the board, none of the wood is cut away and the board lasts a long time. For those who cannot get or make this type of board, a sheet of hardboard makes a good substitute. This can be discarded and replaced with a new piece when it gets too cut. Take care not to press too hard on the knife and do not cut too deeply into the board. A deep cut can deflect the knife the next time round, and can cause damage to the work, not to mention the fingers!

Paring or skiving is usually done on a marble or other smooth, hard service, ideally with a curved edge facing the worker to prevent damage to the work. Plate glass is a good substitute, and a rounded strip of wood can be positioned along the front edge of this, to avoid marking the leather on the edge. Choose a piece of quadrant wooden beading the same thickness as the glass for this.

It is wise to use a separate block of wood for punching holes, setting eyelets or press-studs, as hole punches and other tools of this type can make holes in the cutting board if tapped too hard. These cause uneven cutting over the board, resulting in ragged edges.

Line and Stitch Markers

In order to get accurate, straight and curved stitch lines, and evenly spaced stitches, the leather is always marked out before beginning to sew. This is done in two stages.

The bone folder is used first, to draw lines along which the stitches will be made. This serves two purposes – to act as a guide line for the stitch marker, and to make a shallow groove for the stitches to lie in, to protect them

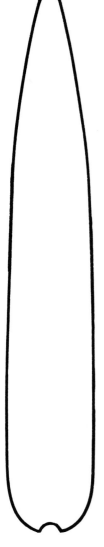

Bone folder with filed niche in the rounded end

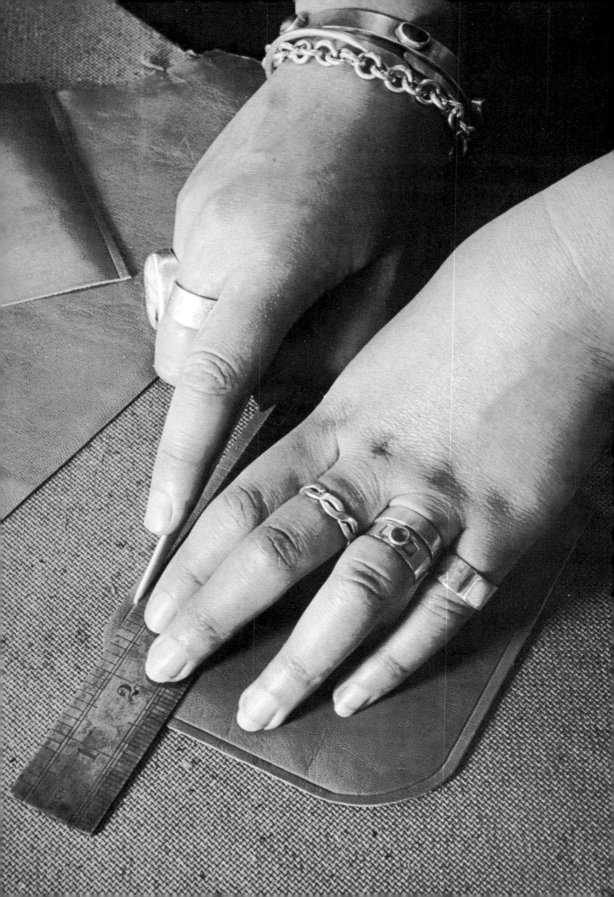

from wear. Bone folders can be brought in different lengths I find that one about 6in long is suitable for most purposes. The pointed end is used for marking, whilst the rounded end is useful for a great many jobs. If you file a small round niche in this, as shown in the diagram, it makes a useful edge burnisher or polisher.

Stitch holes are always marked on the right side of the leather, unless you are stitching a seam from the inside. There are two types of stitch marker – the stitch wheel, and the prong type which is sometimes called a pricking iron. The wheel marker is rather similar to a dressmaker's tracing wheel. It is wheeled along the stitching line and the teeth make small, evenly spaced marks. The pricking iron looks like a small flattened fork with sharp-bladed, angled prongs. These prongs are placed along the stitch line and the top of the tool is tapped lightly with a mallet. The prongs are for marking, not piercing, the leather so care must be taken not to hit too hard. Pricking irons are made in different sizes for different lengths of stitch and the number stamped on the side indicates the number of stitches to the inch. It is usual to make about eight or ten stitches to the inch for handbags, whilst smaller items such as purses or wallets would have about ten or twelve, and briefcases and larger bags a mere six or seven. The price of these tools varies according to the number of prongs they have, not the number of stitches to the inch. A four- or five-pronged tool is the most useful for straight lines, plus a two-pronged one for turning corners. When using the tool, the last prong is inserted in the end hole already made, so as to get even spacing throughout the seam. Pricking irons are usually made by hand and are quite expensive. The best way to build up a collection is to buy one at a time for the particular job in hand.

When stitch positions are marked, an awl is used to pierce them through ready for sewing. This is usually done, a few at a time, whilst stitching. The piercing awl is often called the diamond awl because of the diamond-shaped, very sharp-bladed point. The haft or handle of the awl is held in the palm of the hand with the forefinger pointing down the blade. The angle of the blade must be consistent with the angle of the marked stitches, and all pierced holes must be the same distance from the edge of the work on both sides of the seam to give a neat, even line of stitches.

Marking a seam line with a bone folder and ruler

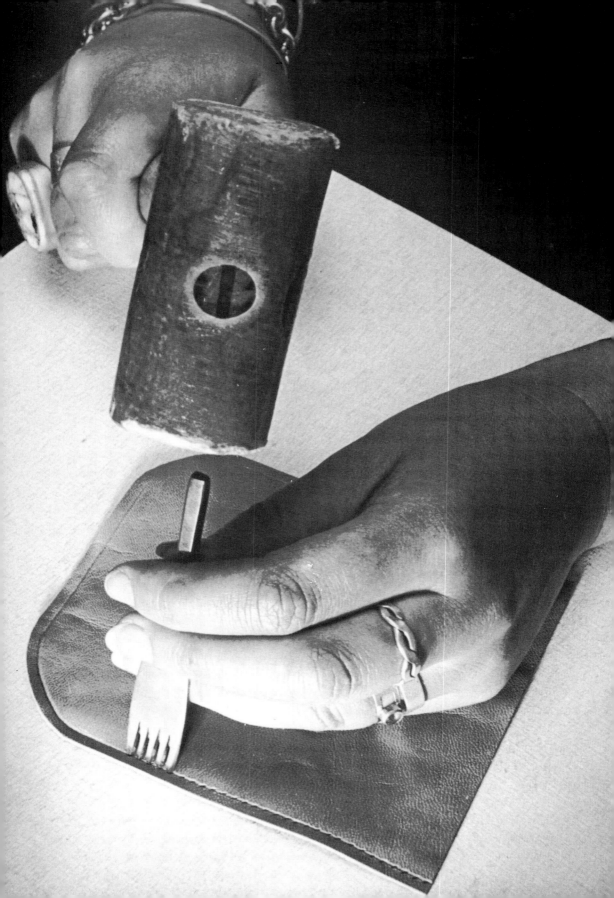

Where a seam is sewn on the inside, then turned right way out after stitching, a tool called a race is used to cut a shallow groove for the stitches to lie in. This is not necessary for thin, supple leathers but if you are working with a thick hide, the thickness could prevent the seam from lying flat inside whatever you are making and this could look bulky from the outside. The race is drawn

Groove made with a race to make the seam lie flat

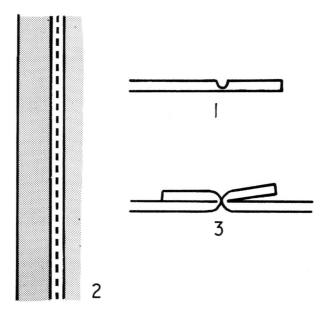

along all seam lines so that the curved blade cuts away about half the thickness of the leather (1). The stitches are then made in this groove (2); then the seam can be made to lie flat (3). You can buy a double-ended race which has different-sized blades at each end for varying thicknesses of leather.

Creasers are used to mark decorative lines in the surface of the leather. They come in a wide range of shapes and sizes, but for the beginner the screw creaser is the most useful. This has two blades which are set by means of a screw to the desired distance apart. The creaser is used to mark a line parallel to the edge of the leather, by positioning it so that one blade runs along the edge whilst the other draws a line just inside. Sometimes a pleasant effect is obtained by heating the screw creaser in a spirit flame before drawing the lines. This makes the line darker in

Marking stitching lines with a pricking iron and mallet

25

colour and also serves, to some extent, to burnish the cut edge of the leather. Remember that damp leather will tend to scorch or burn, so the temperature of the creaser should always be tried out on an offcut before committing it to the real thing.

Adhesives

Different types of adhesive should be used for varying types of leather and join, so you will have to decide the kind of join you need. Will it have to be pliable or rigid? What kind of strain will it have to take? Will it be subject to much dampness during use?

For hard, rigid joins, animal or fish glues are the traditional adhesives. These can, however, be messy, as some of them need to be soaked, then heated in a glue-kettle or double-saucepan and used while still warm. Some of the modern epoxy-resins, such as those employed for woodworking, are successful, too, on hard leathers. The main thing to remember is to give them plenty of time to set and to clamp or weight the pieces together while the adhesive is drying.

Instant adhesion can be obtained by using an impact adhesive, but care must be taken here to get the surfaces placed together correctly the first time or they will stick in the wrong position. This type of adhesive is helpful for holding joins in place while you stick them.

For pliable joins which need to be strong but flexible, a rubber solution is best. Rubber solutions are divided into two kinds—spirit solutions and natural latex adhesives. The spirit rubber solutions are similar in use to impact adhesives in that they dry very quickly by evaporation, so jars and tubes must be kept firmly closed when not needed. The surfaces to be joined should be roughened slightly before a solution is applied in order to give greater penetration. The adhesive is then spread on to both surfaces and left until the spirit has evaporated, before the pieces are accurately pressed into position. The best way to apply a spirit-type solution is to spread it with a small palette knife or plastic spreader. A brush is useless since it quickly gets clogged.

The latex type of rubber solution is usually white in colour when applied, but this alters to semi-transparent as it dries. You can wait for this change to take place before pressing both the treated surfaces together to make an instant bond, or you can just paste one surface and join the sections while the glue is still wet, clamping or weighting them in place. This adhesive can be applied with a small, stiff bristle brush, but it must be washed out immediately afterwards in clean, warm water to prevent clogging. Latex adhesive is sometimes supplied in a jar with the brush attached to the inside of the lid. In this case the brush will not need washing, but the lid should be replaced immediately and screwed down firmly.

Water-bound white paste is generally used for sticking linings in place. It can be thinned down with water if necessary, and care should be taken to remove lumps which would show through the lining. This type of adhesive should not be used where a finished item will be subject to any degree of dampness as it is water-soluble.

Of the many different types of adhesive on the market today, most can be used for leather. Generally speaking, I would advise you to use the types you get on best with, following the instructions on the tube, can or jar. Always test first on an offcut, to see that there is no discolouration of the leather; then try the join for strength and flexibility, and if satisfied, go ahead and use the adhesive.

Needles and Threads

As the stitch holes are made before you begin to sew, there is no need for a sharp-pointed needle. The best needles for most leatherwork are therefore blunt ones with rounded points and largish eyes. Blunt points prevent deflection away from the ready-pierced hole, or splitting and weakening the opposite thread when stitching with two needles. Harness needles are the most commonly used. They are blunt pointed with egg-shaped eyes to make threading easy and are similar to sharps which are the usual needles for most everyday sewing of fabrics. Different sizes are used for different thicknesses of thread and leather to be sewn, and these vary from a No 8 fine to a No o large. I have found that the most useful size for most small objects is the No 5, which is about medium length and thickness. When harness needles are not readily available, ordinary sharps can be adapted for use with leather by rounding off their points on an emery board.

Thread must be strong and should be waxed before use. This is done for two reasons: to help it slide easily through the leather, and to protect the stitching from wear. To wax the thread hold a piece of beeswax in one hand then, starting at one end, draw the thread sharply across the wax several times so that the thread bites into the wax. The waxed thread should feel slightly stiff and should squeak when it is pulled through the fingers. It will also be easier to pass through the eye of the needle.

For most hand sewing on small leather objects the best thread is button thread in either linen or silk. Most colours can be obtained in silk and several basic ones in linen. Button thread can also be obtained now in Polyester, but this sometimes tends to unravel itself during stitching. If you are unable to obtain the colour of thread you need, linen thread can be successfully stained before it is waxed by passing it through a pad soaked in the appropriate colour stain. Remember to stain enough for the whole job before starting as it is difficult to match the strength of colour. For sewing thicker leather, carpet thread and sail-maker's twine can be used .

Remember that the correct needle for the thread is the one with an eye which the thread only just passes through.

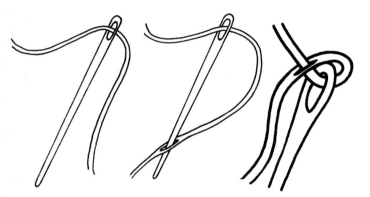

Knotting thread in the eye of a needle

Avoid using too large a needle since there is no sense in enlarging the stitch hole for a fine thread. It is a good idea to anchor the thread in the eye of the needle before beginning to sew. This is done by threading the needle in the usual way, but drawing only a couple of inches through the eye. Twist the main thread just below the needle to unravel it, then pass the needle between the strands and pull the short end until the thread knots just below the eye as shown.

28

Hole Punches

To make neat round or oval holes in items such as belts and straps a punch is used. The most useful kind for the beginner to buy is the six-way plier punch. This has six round punches on a revolving drum; they range from about $\frac{3}{32}$in to about $\frac{1}{4}$in in diameter, and are suitable for use with most firm-textured leathers. Thinner, supple leathers are more difficult to punch as they tend to pucker and get crushed. A useful tip when punching holes in thin leather is to place a small piece of thin card over the leather, on the cutting side, before punching the hole. Individual hole punchers can be bought in different shapes and sizes, and these are needed where the holes to be punched are too far from the edge of the leather for the plier punch to reach. Their structure is basically a hollow tube with one end sharpened to a cutting edge. They are placed on the leather and tapped smartly with a mallet or hammer.

Eyelet and Press-stud Tools

For inserting eyelets a similar plier-action tool can be obtained and used in conjunction with different-sized eyelets. Alternatively a more simple combined hole-and-eyelet tool can be bought which is used with a mallet or hammer in the same way as the individual hole puncher. I have always found this tool much easier to use and more reliable than the complicated plier-action tool. Press-stud tools consist of two punches, one male and one female, for setting the different sides of the press-studs. They are used in the same way as the individual hole-and-eyelet punches. You can buy a wide range of different eyelets, press-studs and decorative studs from the haberdashery departments of large stores. They are usually pre-packed with the tools needed to attach them.

Thonging Tools

Although I have not given any patterns for thonged or laced articles in this book, you may wish to use this method of joining leather for your own designs. The tools needed are fairly simple. For making the slits a cutter which is shaped like a large stitch marker is required; also a thonging needle. The cutter has evenly spaced prongs running in a straight line; it is tapped with a mallet or hammer fairly sharply so that it pierces right through the leather.

You can also use a round punch for making holes for thonging if you prefer the more decorative effect this produces. The thonging needle has a sprung fastener in the eye to hold the end of the thong firmly in place while you are working. Leather lacing or thonging can be bought ready made or you can cut your own from offcuts of suitable leather. A long strip is made by cutting a circle (it does not have to be perfectly round) in a spiral fashion to the centre. You may find the centre part is too curved to use, but the main part of the strip can be pulled out straight and used to lace shapes together.

Other Tools
There are, of course, many other leatherwork tools but, as this book is really aimed at the beginner in leather-work, I have not included any more. All the items shown in the patterns section were made using the tools described in this chapter, so start off by buying just the ones you need for a particular job. As you progress, you will need others so it is worthwhile sending off for a catalogue illustrating the various tools and their uses.

A WORD OF CAUTION Do take care, if there are children in the house, not to leave edge tools and bottles of dye lying about.

Leatherwork Methods and Techniques

Patterns must be made for every part of the item you make; even the simplest shapes should have a pattern or template. Where you intend to cut out two identical pieces, make two patterns to enable you to plan the arrangement of shapes on to the leather with the least amount of wastage before cutting. Where only one shape has to be cut out, stiff paper is usually suitable for a pattern, but if you have to cut three or four, cut out the pattern also from stiff card. Use paper patterns for working out the layout on the leather, then use the stiff template for cutting around with the knife. In cases where a great many similar shapes are required, thin sheet metal may be more suitable for the templates. Professional leather-workers use sheet zinc, which can be cut with straight and curved tin-snips, and smooth the rough edges with emery cloth. If similar shapes are used for the right- and left-hand sides of something, remember to reverse one pattern and write 'left' or 'right' clearly on each one to prevent any mistakes.

If you are designing your own pattern, it is a good idea cut out all shapes from thin card first and assemble them wherever possible to see if the idea really works. Minor adjustments can be made to the working model

31

before starting on the real thing. Remember to allow enough for seam allowances: pieces can always be trimmed smaller, but if you forget to add the seam allowance, nothing can be done once the shapes are cut.

BUYING THE LEATHER

When you are satisfied that the pattern you have made is accurate, you can choose the leather most suitable for making it up. This is an important decision, the finished appearance of the whole project being spoilt if you choose the wrong material. Think of the type of wear the item is likely to get and choose your leather bearing in mind colour, substance and texture in relation to size and shape. Remember to match up skins if you need more than one; look at them in a really good light to compare the colour and texture. Look carefully, too, for any large marks and flaws which will have to be avoided when cutting out.

It is as well to take your patterns along with you when buying the leather, in order to estimate the amount you will need. If in doubt, buy a little extra; you can always use up the left-overs for something else. Like knitting yarns, leather is tanned and dyed in batches and one batch may vary quite considerably from the next. You may be able to arrange with the supplier to hold an extra skin in stock for you for a couple of days if you are really uncertain of the quantity you need.

CUTTING OUT

The next important stage is the cutting out. Accuracy in this is essential and cutting must be planned methodically before you start. The most attractive part of the leather should be selected for the front, top or most visible part of whatever you are making, the strongest part for the area which will get most wear, and the most supple part for places which need to be pliable and soft during use. Large flaws and marks should be avoided, and small marks can go to areas which will not show too much in the finished article. Draw a chalk ring round the inperfections you wish to avoid so that it is easier to see them clearly when planning your cutting out.

The thickest and strongest part of any skin or hide is the area down the centre back from head to tail, and the softest, most pliable and stretchy part is the belly or the side edges. If you are using leather which has an embossed pattern, see that the grain is running in the same direction on all sections of the work, and draw arrows on your paper patterns to indicate the direction of the grain.

Place all pattern pieces on the right side of the skin and mark around them with chalk, a soft pencil or a bone folder, whichever you prefer. Never use a ballpoint or fibre-tipped pen as the ink can seep down into the surface of the leather and permanently stain it. Take your time in working out the most economical layout and double-check left and right pieces and direction of grain before starting to cut.

Cut out all shapes with a sharp knife, using a ruler for the straight edges and taking care to keep the knife blade at right angles to the surface of the leather to avoid under-cutting. This is most important on the thicker leathers where the cut edge will show clearly if it is not quite straight.

Linings and some very thin leathers can be cut with leather shears or very sharp scissors, but never use these where you plan to leave the cut edge exposed, because they do tend to tear the leather rather than cut it cleanly.

SKIVING

Edges and seams which would be clumsy if left to their original thickness should next be skived or pared down ready for sticking or sewing. This is a skill which takes a little time and practice to master thoroughly and I suggest you try it out first on a few offcuts.

Skiving is done on a smooth, hard surface such as stone or glass. I use a piece of plate glass which was once a bathroom shelf. The skiving knife is held firmly in one hand as shown in the photograph whilst the other hand holds the leather steady on the cutting surface. The knife is pushed down, away from the worker towards the edge of the leather, taking off a thin paring and leaving a clean, thin edge. The cut can be tapered gradually or stepped down, depending on what it is to be used for. Firm, thick and rather hard-textured leathers are much easier to skive than the softer, more stretchy ones, so bear this in mind when selecting your leather.

MARKING STITCHING LINES

When all the shapes are cut out and skived, stitch posit-

ions should be marked out ready for sewing. First make a shallow groove along all the stitch lines with a bone folder using a ruler for all the straight lines. This serves two purposes; it provides a clear line to follow with your stitch marker, and it protects the stitches that sink down into it. When all the lines are marked, select a suitably sized pricking iron and mark the stitches along all lines, doing the corners and curved parts first to get them correctly matched.

STICKING AND SEWING

All pieces are now ready for joining with adhesive and/or thread. Choose a suitable adhesive and apply it sparingly. If you intend to have exposed cut edges in the finished work, take care not to get any adhesive on them during the making up, since this may prevent successful burnishing or polishing later on. Stick the sections together as you go along – don't assemble all parts at once – because, while you are sewing, some of the parts you are not working on could become damaged. Larger sections can be pierced through the stitch holes at intervals and tied together with thread, thus preventing undue stress on the adhesive when you are stitching.

PIERCING STITCH HOLES

Different people prefer different ways of working. I usually pierce about eight holes at a time, then sew them and go on to the next eight. You may prefer to pierce one at a time, or a whole straight run, the main thing being to work the way that suits you best. Hold the diamond awl in the palm of the hand with the index finger pointing down the blade. Turn the blade to an angle to correspond with that of the marked stitches and keep this angle consistent throughout so that the line of stitches is straight on both sides of the seam. Watch your fingers on the opposite hand too; the diamond awl is extremely sharp and can be most painful!

DIFFERENT STITCHES

Saddle-stitch

This is a method of sewing using two blunt-pointed harness needles. Saddle-stitching makes a very attractive seam which is neat and even on both sides; it is used for all seams where both sides will be clearly visible. The leather

Cutting out leather shapes using a set-square as a guide to accurate corners

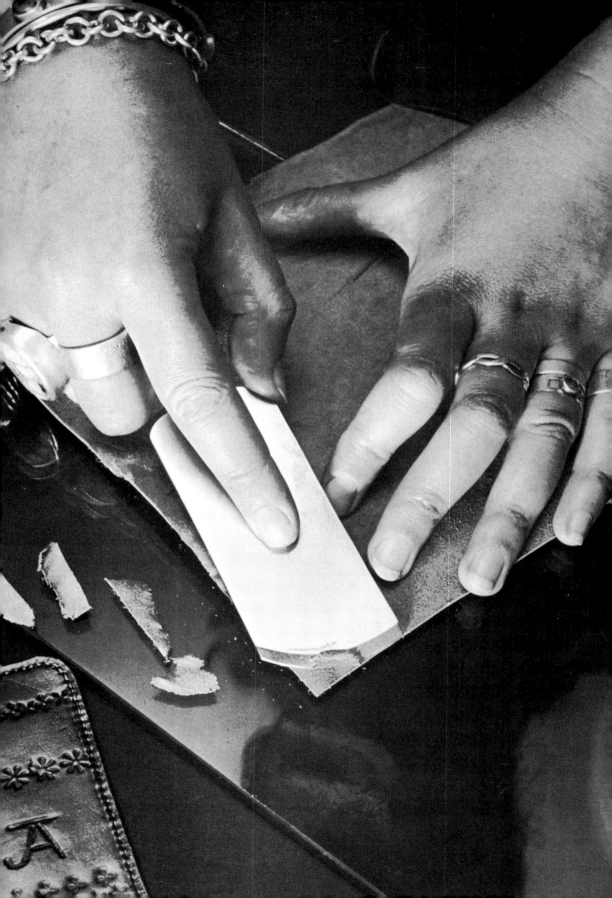

needs to be held, either by a bench or knee clamp or, if it is a large item, between the knees, thus leaving both hands free to sew. First pierce a number of stitch holes, then cut a length of thread just over twice as long as the seam if it is a fairly short seam (otherwise you will have to join threads later on). Wax the thread thoroughly and thread each end on to a harness needle, anchoring the ends in the eyes as described on p28. Pass one needle through the second pierced hole from the right and draw the thread through until equal lengths extend to each needle. Holding one needle in each hand, push the right-hand needle through the end hole and, when the point emerges, insert the left-hand needle in the same hole just below and in front of the first needle (see diagram). Push both needles

Saddle-stitch

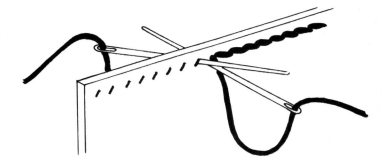

through the hole and pull the threads taut. Continue sewing from right to left, always inserting the right-hand needle first. This will give you a line of consistently slanting stitches which look attractive on both sides of the seam. To finish off a line of stitching, stitch backwards through three or four holes, then cut off the ends of the thread close to the work.

Backstitch

Where only one side of a seam will show, for example when stitching a pocket on to a bag, backstitch can be used instead of saddle-stitch. The holes are pierced in the same way, but only one needle is used to sew a single continuous line of stitches on one side and a double line on the other.

Stab-stitch

Ordinary running-stitch cannot be used on leather

Skiving the edge of the leather with a skiving knife to make it thinner before sewing. Note the position of the left hand holding the leather down on to the glass

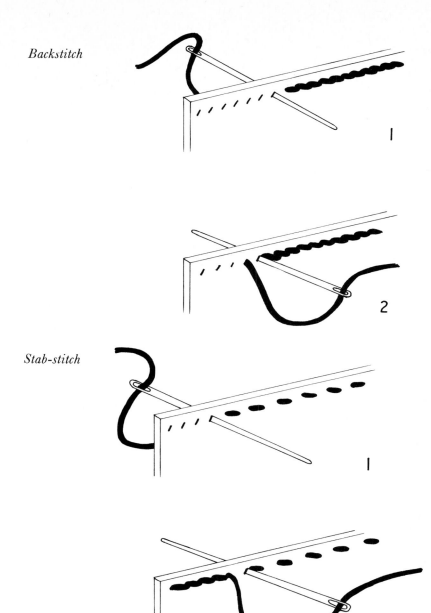

Backstitch

1

2

Stab-stitch

1

2

Saddle-stitching a seam using two harness needles. Note the improvised knee-clamp to hold the work. This is made from two pieces of hardboard and some large bulldog clips

because of the distortion which would occur. A similar effect can, however, be produced with stab-stitching. Pierce the holes with the awl, then simply pass the needle and thread in and out of alternate holes as shown in the diagram. For an extra-strong seam and one which looks rather like saddle-stitching, stab-stitch the seam again, but this time going the reverse way through the holes (2).

GLOVING NEEDLES

If you are using very thin supple leathers, a gloving needle can be used instead of the diamond awl for piercing and stab-stitching in one operation. Always choose a small-sized needle to avoid making large holes in the leather. If you plan to restitch this seam as described above, replace the gloving needle with a harness needle, or the gloving needle, being very sharp bladed, will cut through your existing stitches.

LINING

Separate pieces of pattern are usually lined individually before being made up. Remember that skiver is easily torn, so treat it with care. Remember also that any lumps of adhesive, ends of threads, etc will show through the skiver if they inadvertently get stuck between it and the main leather, so keep the bench free of trimmings while you stick down the lining. Apply paste to the main leather, place the lining flat on the table with the wrong side uppermost, then bring the main leather down on to it. Turn the whole section over to ascertain that there are no creases in the lining, but do not rub or stretch or it will shrink again when the adhesive dries and distort the shape. Place a flat weight on the lined part until it dries.

EDGES

There are two main types of finished edges in leatherwork; these are 'cut edge' and 'turned edge'. Cut edge work is mainly used for straps, folios, purses, and many small, hard leather items. It is a simple technique to master and gives a firm, clean finished look to the edge of the work. Turned edge work is more sophisticated and rather more difficult to master. Unlike cut edge work, it necessitates skiving the edges before turning and sticking or sewing in place. This must be practised in order to get a uniform thickness of the edge and therefore a smooth fold. It is used for high quality wallets, bags, purses and other items which require a highly finished look.

Cut Edge Work

As the name implies, this method leaves the cut edge of the leather exposed. This is then stained if necessary and burnished or polished. The most important part of the procedure is accurate cutting out to begin with, as it is difficult to trim off any irregularities from an otherwise straight edge without making the problem worse. If the item you are making has smaller pockets or tabs attached to it, the edges of these should be finished off before assembling them because they are easier to reach at this stage. Where the colour of the cut edge is too pale in comparison with the surface of the leather, it can be coloured with an appropriate stain, let down with water, then burnished while still damp. This is done by rubbing with a pinching action between the forefinger and thumb. The moisture closes the fibres of the leather and gives it a smooth shiny edge. Vegetable-tanned leathers burnish very well, but some chrome-tanned ones are not so suitable for cut edge work. The chrome-tanning process makes them more waterproof, and the fibres do not respond in the same way to the moisture. Always try out a small offcut first to see how it will react. Take care not to get any adhesive on the cut edge during assembly, since this may seal the edge against the moisture. It is a good idea to use a water-soluble adhesive for this type of work; then the adhesive can be wiped away with a damp cloth before staining and burnishing. For a decorative line around the edge of articles, the screw creaser can be used in conjunction with the cut edge.

Turned Edge Work

This is generally used where the item is to be lined. The edges of the main leather are skived, the lining is stuck in place minus the seam allowances, then the edge of the leather is turned back and folded down over the edge of the lining. The most important part of this operation is the preparation of the skived edge, which must be pared down very evenly before sticking the lining in place. When you have cut out your shapes, draw in the seam allowance on the flesh side, then skive this away gradually until the very edge of the leather is paper thin. This is something you must practise until you know by sight and feel whether it is skived sufficiently for a smooth fold. Paste the main part of the leather and stick the trimmed lining in place.

41

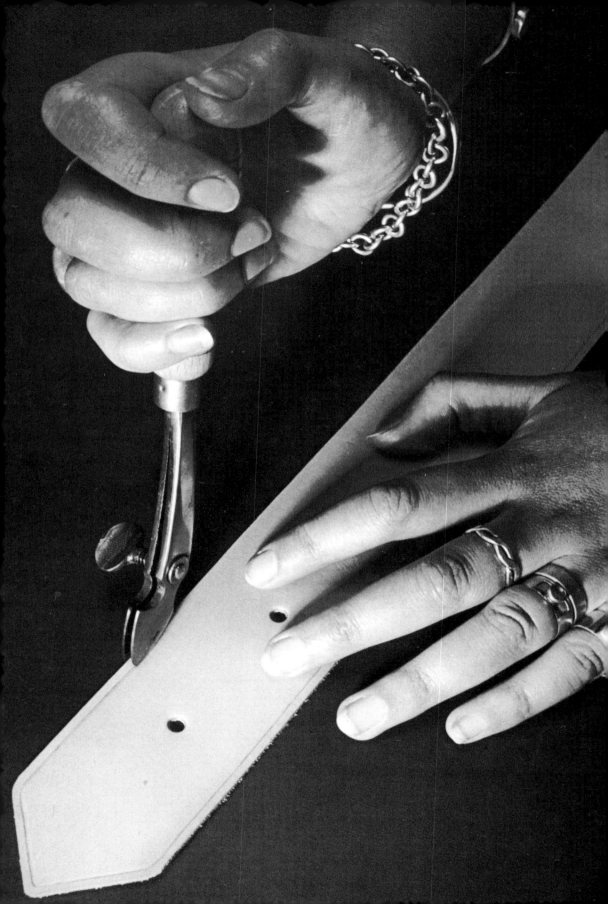

Weight this and allow it to dry thoroughly before turning over the edges of the main leather and sticking them in place. Apply the adhesive sparingly to the skived edges, because if you apply too much it will ooze out from under the turned edge and discolour the lining. Weight the lined section and the turned edge and allow the adhesive to dry thoroughly before stitching. Sometimes stitching is not necessary, but if the article is likely to get a lot of wear or be subject to any dampness which could affect the adhesive, it is as well to stitch the hem for extra strength.

CORNERS

Generally speaking, as a pointed corner will wear out much quicker than a rounded one it is a good idea to round off the corners wherever possible. In cut edge work this presents no problem, since the edges are just trimmed to the shape you want and stained and burnished in the usual way. Problems start to occur with turned edge work, however, because there is invariably more skived edge to turn in than there is lining to stick it to. There are two ways of overcoming this; you can either take small pleats or tucks in the skived edge, folding them all the same way for neatness, or you can clip out little pieces from the edge and mitre the remaining sections together. This second method will make a flatter and smoother edge in the finished work, but it is a little more difficult to execute, because of the accuracy needed in clipping out the pieces.

PIPING

Piping is used for larger, heavier leather items such as suitcases and holdalls. It is used for seams which are stitched on the wrong side and then turned right side out when finished. It makes an excellent corner for right-angled surfaces where it takes the worst of any wear and tear, and strengthens the seams.

The process is the same as piping in dressmaking or soft furnishing, except that piping cord is not generally used. A strip of leather is cut to the length of the seam and folded in half lengthwise (1), then the two sides are stuck together with adhesive and the strip is inserted between the seams (2), and stitched firmly in place through all layers. When the article is turned right side out the folded edge of the piping forms the corner of the seam (3).

Finishing the edges of a plain belt with a screw-creased line

43

To join strips of leather to make a long piece of piping, cut the ends diagonally (4), then skive the flesh side of one and the grain side of the other until they are tapered

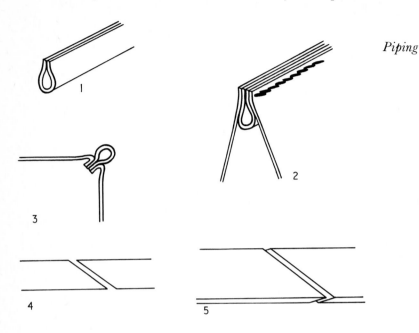

Piping

to a similar thickness. Overlap them and stick carefully in place (5). Use a good strong adhesive for this and, when placing piping in a seam, make sure that no joins like this occur on the curved corners of the finished article, in case the adhesive fails and the join begins to gape.

RIGHT-ANGLED MITRED CORNERS

When making right-angled corners in rigid leather as for boxes or shoe-brush cases, the two sections can be cut with mitred edges so that they fit together exactly. They are glued firmly in place then stitched diagonally through the corner (1). This makes a very strong seam. If you want an invisible seam on a corner like this, cut a diagonal slit a short distance from the corner (2), then insert the stitches in this slit and glue it closed.

POCKETS

The small pockets in handbags, designed to hold a mirror, are the most simple type to make since they need no gusset. A rectangle of thin leather or double skiver, a little larger than the mirror, is simply stitched in place to the

44

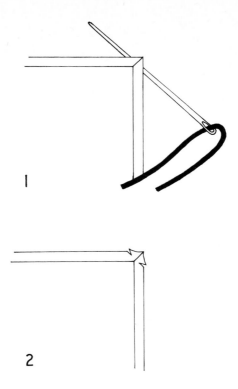

1

2

lining around the sides and base before the bag is assembled. If you are making a pocket of this type from skiver, cut a piece twice as deep as the mirror plus seam allowances, then fold this in half and stick it back to back to make the double thickness. Remember that it will probably shrink a little after pasting, so allow some extra and trim it to the exact size when it has dried. When this is stitched to the inside of the lining, the folded edge of the skiver forms the top edge of the pocket.

Outside pockets on a bag are usually made from the same leather as the bag, and their method of construction depends on the style of the bag and the size of the pocket. For example, a cut edge work bag could have a small simple patch pocket just stitched on to the front, whilst a more sophisticated, turned edge bag would need a pocket which was lined and probably gussetted.

The easiest way of making a gusset is to fold a small pleat at either side (1), then stitch the pocket in place around the sides and lower edge. Another way of making a pocket to hold larger items is to cut a separate gusset strip and sew this around the sides and base (2). The other

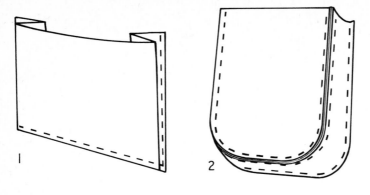

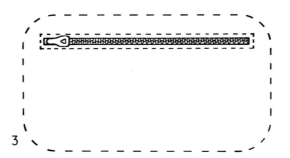

side of the strip is then sewn to the bag. This type of pocket can be attached to the outside of a bag for carrying a purse so that you do not have to keep opening and closing the bag. It would be wise in this case to include a top flap of some sort to keep the contents safely inside.

Another way of making a safe pocket is to cut a slit in the front of the bag and stitch a zip-fastener into it, then place a shaped piece of leather behind this and stitch in place around the edges (3). The stitching that holds this type of pocket in place will show from the outside of the bag, so it is a good idea to make a decorative feature of it by stitching in contrast thread, or perhaps by making several parallel lines of stitches. You could even make the pocket an unusual outline shape, bearing in mind that whatever is inside must be easily accessible.

HANDLES AND STRAPS

The simplest type of handle is a straight strap, the length and width of this depending on the weight and size of the

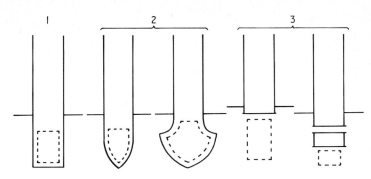

item and how it is to be carried. Think about how comfortable the chosen width of strap is in your hand – a thin one will cut and one that is too thick will crease and fold. Shoulder-straps should also be tried out in the same way.

To make a strap to use with a cut edge work item, simply cut a strip of leather to the desired size and burnish the long edges. You can, if you wish, screw-crease a line down each side for extra decoration, or you can cut double the length you need and stick or sew it, back-to-back to make it stronger and reversible. For turned edge work it is better to make a turned edge strap, and the neatest way to do this is to cut a strip of leather twice as wide as you will need it. Skive the flesh side of this for a quarter of its width down each long side, then fold it sides-to-middle down its length and firmly stick in place. If desired, you can stitch this turning for extra strength, particularly if it is to get a lot of wear.

The next part of the procedure is to attach the strap to the bag or whatever you are making, This can be done in several ways. You can stitch the ends in place with strong thread (1), or you can shape the ends first (2), to make a decorative feature of them. For a neater effect a slit can be made in the bag and the handle inserted into this before being stitched in place. This can also be turned into a decorative feature (3) as well as making the handle a little more stable.

These are just ideas for stitching the handle in place, but you can also use different metal attachments. If you fit your handle to a ring of some sort it will be able to move slightly during use and this will to some extent prevent undue strain on the handle. Round rings, D rings and rectangular rings can be used for this, and they are normally attached to the bag by means of a short strap

the same width as the main handle. This can be plain or
decorative as you wish (4). Another neat way of attaching
this type of handle is to use a metal handle loop which is

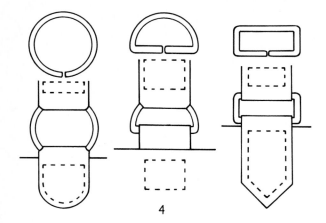

*Attaching a handle to a bag
with a ring*

inserted into a slit in the bag rather like a rivet. The tabs
go through a washer, then open out inside the bag to
make a strong fastening (5). This is really suitable for the
heavier leathers which will not pull out of shape.

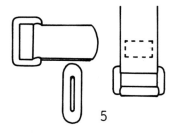

*Attaching a handle with a
metal hand loop*

So much for strap handles. Some of the heavier bags,
however, will need a thicker handle which is more
comfortable to hold. These usually need to be padded in
some way to give them the necessary extra bulk. A fairly
easy type of handle to make is one which uses a
thick cord encased within a leather strap: the stages of
making this are shown in diagram 6. A length of thick
cord is stuck in place to the centre of the wrong side of a
strip of leather with spear-shaped ends. This is then
wrapped around the cord and stitched in place close to
the edges of the leather. The shaped ends of the handle
are then opened out slightly to make an attractive curved

Making a handle by encasing a thick cord within a leather strap

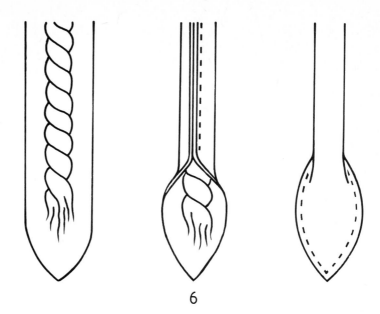

6

shape, and stitched firmly in place to the bag. This sort of handle can also be attached by means of a ring (7). This gives greater flexibility to the handle and allows it to fall away from the bag when not being held, thus

A cord and leather handle attached by a ring

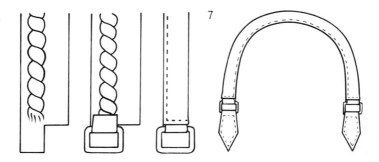

7

making it easier in some instances to gain access to the inside of the bag.

To attach strap-handles to the top of a bag or case, neat metal handle plates (8) can be bought, or the handle can be attached by means of a leather strap passing through a slit in the top of the article and stitched firmly in place inside (9).

49

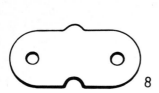 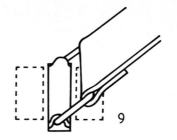

FASTENINGS

There are so many different ways of fastening that it is often very difficult to choose one for a particular item. Think first about how often the fastening will be used; then decide whether you want it to be a decorative feature or as unobtrusive as possible, then choose the fastening for its practical application as well as its looks.

To start with, consider the types of fastening which are made from the leather itself and which have no metal fittings. The flap part of a bag pocket might need a fastening of some sort to keep its contents secure and this could be made very simply, as shown in diagram 1. The

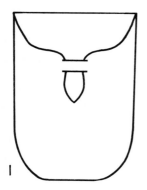 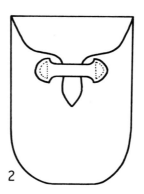

Two strap fastenings

flap of the pocket has been shaped into a strap, then a slot has been cut in the front of the pocket itself for this to slide through. The second fastening illustrated is a little more sophisticated – a shaped bar of leather has been stitched in place to hold the strap down. A similar simple fastening can be made by cutting a slot in the pocket flap and threading something through this as you would thread a button through a buttonhole. This could be shaped in a very decorative way to make a prominent

50

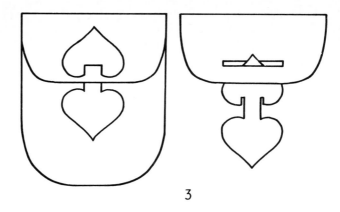

3

feature of it (3). Similarly, a leather toggle (4) could be made to pass, through a slit, or a leather loop, to make a kind of rustic button and buttonhole (5).

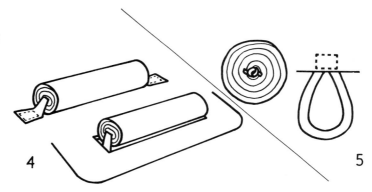

4   5

For more sophisticated articles, zip-fasteners and press-studs can be used, and these are simple enough not to need any real explanation. Press-studs can be attached to the individual pieces of the item before it is made up, or left until last, depending on whether they are easy to get at and whether or not you will want to leave the item weighted for any time. A press-stud might leave a permanent indented mark on the article, so it is best left until last.

Buckles and straps can be a very attractive form of fastening, and they blend particularly well with leather. Of the many different types of fashion buckles available nowadays, some are suitable for use with leather. Attractive old buckles can also often be found in secondhand and junk shops, and can sometimes be bought for just a few pence. Old harness buckles look most attractive on some heavier leather articles; they usually have well-proportioned shapes, as well as being extremely functional.

Where a buckle will have to take a lot of strain, for example on a bulging bag or case, it is best to use one with a roller which helps the strap to roll through it so preventing unnecessary wear. These are made in both single and double shapes (6). The single shapes usually need some kind of leather 'keep' to hold the strap down firmly in place.

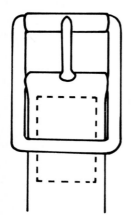
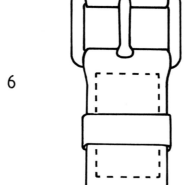

6

A double and a single roller buckle

If the leather you are using is thick and firm you will need only to punch a hole in it to take the prong of the buckle, but where softer and thinner leather is used you should reinforce the hole with an eyelet, choosing either brass, nickle, or a colour to tone in with both the leather and the buckle used.

Other buckles have no prongs at all, the simplest of these being a slide buckle which relies on its shape alone to hold the leather in place (7). These can be used for belts where the strap part is pulled straight and fairly taut, but for handles and similar purposes they are not

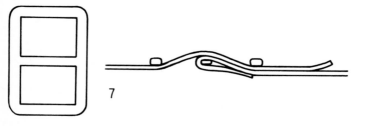

A slide buckle

7

suitable because any movement will cause them to slide down the strap. Another kind of buckle is the clasp type, which consists of two shaped ends which clip together (8). These come in a wide variety of types and designs.

A clasp buckle

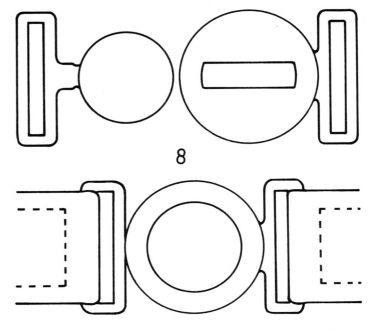

8

The turnlock (9), is another common type of bag fastener. It is inserted into slits cut in the bag and the bag flap rather like a rivet, and has two parts plus two washers. The tabs of the main parts of the lock are pressed through slits cut into the leather, then through the washers, and

A turnlock

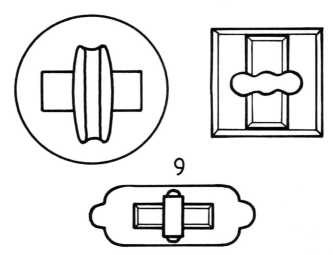

9

bent outwards to secure them in place. Care must be taken to position both parts carefully so that they will fasten accurately without putting undue strain on the lock. Turnlocks are made in different shapes, sizes and degrees of ornament to suit a wide range of bags and purses.

Specific Decorative Effects

There are several methods of imprinting a three-dimensional pattern on to the surface of a smooth leather by hand. Natural hide, calf or sheepskin are the most suitable types of leather for this, being smooth and free from any embossed grains. The leather is dampened first with water to make it pliable, then the pattern is applied. When it dries the leather hardens again and the pattern becomes permanent. Care must be taken not to get the leather too wet in the first place, or it can become too pliable or take ages to dry, and, since it should be dried lying out flat, this could take up valuable working space. To avoid watermarks, always apply the moisture evenly all over with a damp sponge; watermarks occur around the edge of a dampened patch if this does not extend to the edges of the leather. Remember that the shape will shrink a little while it is drying, so cut out a piece a little larger than you need and trim it to the final shape when the work is dry again.

Purchased decorative punches are made from brass or steel, or you can make your own by inserting a screw into a length of dowel and then filing the screw head into a pattern with a jeweller's file. These punches are placed in position on the surface of the leather and tapped with a

55

mallet or hammer. The harder they are hit the deeper the pattern will be, so care must be taken to keep the depth as uniform as possible, especially in repeat patterns. Most of these punches are quite small and so are really most suitable for borders, small repeat patterns or for filling in larger areas of a design to make a textured background.

Larger designs can be drawn freehand on to the face of the leather with a soft pencil or bone folder, then modelled into shape using a variety of modelling tools. These are used to press down some areas of the design, leaving the others to stand out in light relief. Very beautiful and intricate pieces of work can be done in this way; lines,dots, and solid areas can be produced, and decorative punches, as already described, can be used to fill in larger areas of the design in tightly knit repeat patterns.

Repoussé work is done mainly from the reverse side of the leather. A tracing of the design is drawn on transparent paper. The paper is then reversed and the pattern traced on to the flesh side using carbon paper. The dampened leather is then supported in the palm of the hand and the design is pressed on to it from the flesh side with different modelling tools. This makes a raised pattern on the grain side. To emphasise the outlines it is sometimes a good idea to pare away part of the thickness of the leather on the flesh side, but take care not to overdo this or you could end up with rather hard, unpleasant lines. When a sufficiently deep relief has been obtained, the leather is turned over and details added to the right side with modelling tools. Where the finished item is intended to be kept rigid during use the hollows in the flesh side can be filled in with plaster of Paris or papier mâché to help keep the design in shape and prevent damage to it. This is not practical, though, for articles needing to be flexible in use, since the filling would soon crack and break away. Bear in mind that the higher the relief the more damage it is likely to suffer during use; remember also that patterns can easily be overdone and the idea of a design should be to enhance the surface of the leather, not to obliterate it. Try to avoid large, plain areas raised above the surface, as they are not really all that interesting to look at; try to keep designs balanced and attractive all over.

When the leather has dried and been trimmed into shape and made up, a coat of good quality white wax polish will improve the colour and enhance the design as well as protect the surface against shallow scratches. Alternatively you may prefer to colour the design in some way, either in part or all over. Here again, however, do not overdo it; let the grain and texture of the leather show through the design wherever possible.

THONGING AND LACING

Thonging is really a means of sewing with a narrow strip of leather instead of using a thread, in order to make a decorative edge or join. The thongs can be bought ready cut, or you can make your own. The leather for the thongs must be thin and supple, but also fairly strong and not likely to stretch after the article has been made.

Holes or slits have to be punched around the edges of the item to take the thong and this can be done with a special thonging tool which makes slits, or a punch which will make round holes. The holes or slits must be evenly spaced in a line parallel to the edge of the work; the usual distance is between $\frac{1}{4}$in and $\frac{1}{8}$in from the edge, depending on the size of the item you are making. If you are punching round holes, make sure they are small ones just large enough to take the width of the thong; larger ones tend to look untidy and can weaken the edge.

The most usual thonging stitch is simple overcasting which makes a firm decorative edge. This can be used simply as a decoration or to join two layers of leather together. If you are joining two layers in this way, they can first be stuck together around the very edges to hold them securely whilst they are being punched and thonged. The end of the thong is sandwiched between the layers where you start to stitch (1), and then the other end is

Thonging and lacing

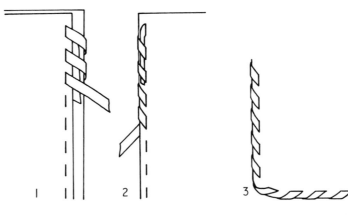

slipped in between the layers and glued firmly in place where you finish. If you are sewing a single layer only, the first end is positioned along the edge of the leather (2) and the stitching worked over it. The final end is pushed back under the last few stitches and glued in place to make both ends look alike.

Corners should be rounded off and the holes or slits arranged in such a way as to ensure that a stitch occurs in the centre of the corner (3). If corners are left pointed and not protected by a central stitch they will tend to curl and bend during use and begin to look rather untidy.

An alternative stitch is running thonging, where the slits are made at right angles to the edge of the work and the thong is threaded alternately in and out of them. Cross-stitch is another simple stitch; the edge is oversewn in one direction, the thong passing through alternate holes or slits, then returning to stitch through the re-maining holes in the opposite direction. This can be done with two different-coloured thongs to give added interest to the decoration. Simple blanket-stitch can also be used, taking care to keep the right side of the thong facing up-wards all the time; this gives an interesting and very firm edge to the work. There are many other ways of decorating an edge by thonging and it is worth experi-menting with different colours and stitches until you obtain the effect you are seeking.

To join strips of thonging to make up sufficient length, cut the ends obliquely, skive them and stick them together in the same way as for piping, then hammer the join well to flatten it. It is wisest to join on extra lengths only as you need them to save pulling yards of thonging through each hole. It is not always necessary to use a thonging needle, some leathers will be stiff enough to thread through the holes without one, particularly if you have made round holes, but you can stiffen the end of the thong with a little glue to assist the threading.

Lacing is used mainly on garments and items where a semi-permanent fastening is needed which can be undone in order to gain access to the inside of the article. The leather for this must be stronger and thicker than thong-ing since it will get more wear, and the holes should be reinforced with eyelets to help keep their shape. Several different lacing stitches can be used, the most common

58

(Left) *Cross-over stitch;*
(right) *straight bar stitch*

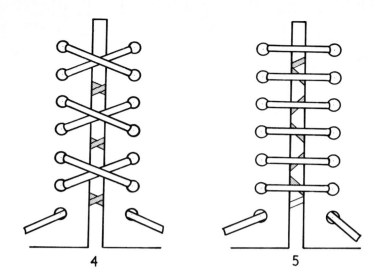

4   5

being a cross-over stitch (4) and a straight bar stitch (5). The ends of laces can be trimmed with small tassels, beads or decorative knots to give added interest.

STAINING AND POLISHING

Leather is available in such a wide variety of colours these days that staining is often only necessary for the edges of some cut edge work and the insides of some small unlined items. Sometimes, however, a special effect is required which can be obtained only if you colour the work yourself. Perhaps you want a two-colour pattern, or wish to add areas of colour to a tooled design.

The best stain to use is an Aniline dye which is bought in powder form and mixed with methylated spirits. Really beautiful, brilliant colours can be obtained in this form, and they will not fade, but care must be taken in their storage and handling. A few grains spilt on your hands or clothes will go unnoticed until they get damp, then bright patches of colour will appear which will not wash out. Different colours can be mixed together provided they are the same type of stain, but take care to mix them thoroughly to avoid a streaky effect. Always try out any stain on an offcut of similar leather first, and practise staining a large offcut before colouring the leather for a large item, so that you evolve a good technique before you start.

If you are staining an edge only, apply the stain with a small brush, giving it two coats if necessary, then burnishing the edge while it is still wet. Where you wish to stain the flesh side of a small article such as a purse, it must be done before the purse is made up, then left to dry before sticking and sewing. Make a pad from a lump of cotton wool in the centre of a piece of rag, twist the rag around the cotton wool to hold it in a firm, hard bundle, then apply the stain sparingly with this in a sharp dabbing motion to get a slightly stippled effect all over. Avoid loading the pad with too much stain or it may bleed through on to the right side of the leather, and do not try to rub it on or you will end up with an untidy streaky effect.

If you plan to stain the grain side of a fairly large item, remember to mix enough stain for the whole job, since it is almost impossible to get exactly the same strength of colour on a second mixing. The stain can be applied either with a large, soft bristled brush, or with a pad of cotton wool and rag as already described, depending on your personal preference. The surface of the leather should be dampened first with methylated spirits to assist even staining, and the first coat of stain should be applied while the leather is still damp. A circular rubbing motion should be used for the first coat, followed by a straight side-to-side motion for the second coat which should be applied immediately, before the first one has time to dry. Small areas of colour on a decorated surface can be applied with a small watercolour brush. Take great care not to overload the brush or it may flood the design and ruin the desired effect.

If you are unable obtain Aniline dyes, most of the stains used for woodworking can be successfully used on leather and, apart from wood tones, bright primary colours are now produced in some ranges. These stains may need diluting so examine the label on the bottle or tin and choose those which are spirit based and can be diluted with methylated spirits. Suede dyes can also be used successfully on some leathers such as natural tooling hide, calf or basil, and of course, suede. The main advantage of these is that they can be bought ready mixed in small quantities.

All grain leather responds well to a coat of good polish, and a colourless wax shoe, floor or furniture polish can be used. The best way of applying polish is with a soft shoe-brush which will not clog the pores of the leather as a cloth might do. A brush is also more efficient at getting into odd corners. Buff up the surface with a piece of mutton-cloth or other soft rag; polish helps to protect the surface from dirt and scratches and it also enhances colours.

Some Things to Make

SIMPLE PURSE

This flat purse is made from four pieces of tan calf which have been stitched together in a way which makes three separate sections inside. The largest part of the purse forms the back and the flap-over front. This is lined with matching skiver. The purse fastens with a press-stud.

Materials
A piece of calf leather about 11in by 8in
A piece of matching skiver about 7in by 4in
Water-bound paste adhesive
Waxed linen thread
A press-stud

Method
Make a pattern from the diagram (scale: one square represents 1sq in) and use this to cut out one shape A, one shape B and two shapes C from the leather. Also cut out one shape A from the skiver. Use a race to cut a shallow groove along the dotted line on the wrong side of piece A to enable it to fold easily over the front of the purse when it is assembled. Carefully paste the flesh side of shape A and line it with the skiver and then leave to dry under a heavy book.

Simple purse and wallet

62

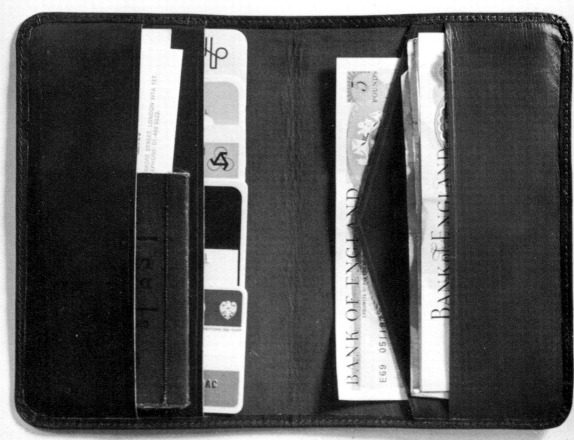

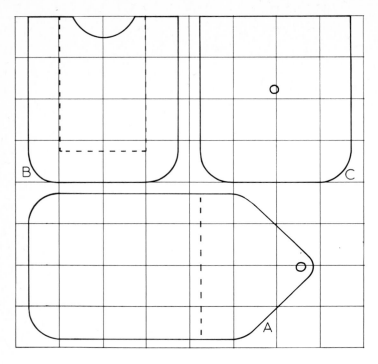

Meanwhile arrange shape B and one shape C with the grain sides facing and stitch them together ¾in from the edges around the sides and base, as indicated by the dotted line on piece B. Using a bone folder and ruler, mark a line around the sides and base of the other piece C on the grain side ⅛in from the edge, curving the line around the corners. When piece A has thoroughly dried, mark a similar line all around it, then use a No 10 pricking iron to mark stitch holes along these lines. Attach one half of a press-stud to the pointed end of piece A and the other half to the centre of piece C, as illustrated by the small circles. Spread a little paste around the very edges of the flesh side of piece B and also the edges of the piece C with the press-stud, place the two sections together with the flesh sides inside and leave to set. When the adhesive is thoroughly dry, pierce the stitch holes through these two sections, taking care not to damage the attached section C, and saddle-stitch them together around the sides and base to make the front section of the purse.

To make the back and front flap, stick the flesh side of section A to the flesh side of section C around the very edges, then when the adhesive is thoroughly dry, saddle-stitch them together continuing the line of stitches around the front flap of the purse. Bend this flap along the grooved line to close the press-stud.

TAN CALF WALLET

This simple wallet would be an excellent first thing to make, since cutting, skiving, pasting, heat creasing and stitching can all be practised on this one item.

Materials
Rectangle of calf $9\frac{1}{2}$in by $7\frac{1}{2}$in
Rectangle of calf 7in by $3\frac{1}{2}$in
Rectangle of calf 7in by 3in
Two rectangles of calf 7in by 2in
Rectangle of matching skiver 9in by 7in
Water-bound paste adhesive
Matching silk or linen thread

Method
Trim all four corners of the largest rectangle of calf into rounded shapes using a $1\frac{1}{2}$in-diameter circle as a template; then carefully skive the flesh side of all the edges and rounded corners to a depth of about $\frac{1}{2}$in, graduating the thickness carefully until the leather is paper thin at the very edge. Paste the flesh side of this piece of calf, round off the corners of the skiver and stick it into place on it, centring the skiver carefully and making sure there are no lumps or wrinkles in it. Leave this section to dry under a heavy book or similar smooth weight. Meanwhile, take the 7in by $3\frac{1}{2}$in rectangle and find the centre of one of the long

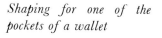
Shaping for one of the pockets of a wallet

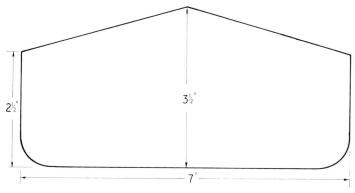

65

sides. Mark this lightly with a pencil at the very edge, then trim this side to a shallow point as shown in the diagram and round off the opposite two corners using a 1in-diameter circle as a template. Also round off two corners of each of the other rectangles to correspond. Very carefully skive the flesh side along the two ends and one side of each of these rectangles, skiving around the curved corners as well so that you will not have too great a thickness to sew through later on. Set a screw creaser to about $\frac{1}{8}$in between the blades and gently heat it, then crease the grain side of the unskived edge of each of the rectangles, including the pointed side of the largest one. When the main part of the wallet has thoroughly dried out, arrange the other sections on to it with the wrong sides together, the two largest first, and the two smaller ones on top. Make sure that all the edges are in line with the outer edges of the main part of the wallet, leaving an equal area of turning all round and trimming off any surplus from the edge of the skiver if necessary. Stick all sections in place around the outside edges and leave to dry. Carefully paste the skived edges of the main part of the wallet and turn these down over the edges of the other assembled parts, making tiny tucks or pleats around the curved corners and pressing them down flat. When the adhesive has dried, the wallet is ready to be stitched around the edge. Do this from the right side of the wallet, noting how deep the turned edge is, and stitching down the centre of the seam allowance. If you like, the stitching can be done with a sewing machine, or it can be done by hand, first ruling a line with a bone folder, marking the stitches with a pricking iron and then piercing with an awl and saddle-stitching all around.

UNDERARM FOLIO WITH ZIP-FASTENER

Choose a good, fairly flawless piece of leather for this folio since there is no decoration to detract from the surface. A generously wide gusset means that you could carry bulky books and paper without distorting the shape of the folio, and it zips open around two and a half sides for easy access (see p120).

Materials
Piece of hide 24in by 18in
Strip of hide 42in by 1$\frac{1}{2}$in

Tooled hide notepad cover

Latex adhesive
Waxed linen thread
36in-long heavy duty zip-fastener

Method
Make sure that the edges of both pieces of leather are cut straight and that the corners are true right angles before you start. Make a cardboard template from a 3in-diameter circle and use this to cut around the corners of the large piece of leather. Make a template from a 1½in-diameter circle and use this to cut around one end of the gusset strip. Carefully cut out a slot from the centre of the gusset as shown in the diagram, starting ½in from the rounded end and continuing to the exact length of the zip-fastener. With a bone folder and ruler, crease a line around this slot ⅛in from the edge, then use a No 6 pricking iron to mark the stitches in this line. Stick the zip-fastener smoothly into this slot, using latex adhesive very sparingly and leave it until thoroughly dry. Then pierce the stitch holes with an awl and saddle-stitch around the zip with waxed thread using harness needles. Crease a line around the edges of the large piece of leather, employing a template for the rounded corners and a ruler for the straight edges, then mark stitches with the pricking iron all around. Fold this main part of the folder in half and lightly mark the centre of the crease on each side. Carefully dampen the rounded end of the gusset and ease it into one side of the fold, sticking in place very sparingly with latex adhesive. Take care not to get any of this adhesive on the cut edges of the leather as it will prevent successful burnishing later on. Continue to stick the gusset in place around the sides of the main part of the folder, damping it and easing it around the corners. When you get to within about 2in of the opposite fold, stop and estimate how much more gusset you will need, then trim off the excess using the 1½in-diameter template. Dampen the end of the gusset and ease carefully into the fold, sticking it in place with latex adhesive. When the gusset is completely in position, pierce the stitch holes with the awl and saddle-stitch it in place with waxed thread. To finish off the folder, burnish the edges with a dampened cloth to give them a hard smooth finish. The gusset can be softened with saddle-soap and the folio polished with a clear wax polish and buffed to a rich shine.

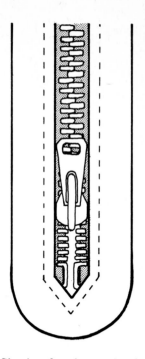

Shaping for zip opening in gusset

This would make an ideal present for someone who is studying and who needs to carry a pad for taking notes. The cover makes the pad firm enough to write on without using a desk or table and it has been designed to fit a standard-size shorthand pad.

Materials

Spiral-wire bound shorthand pad with pages measuring 8in by 5in

Two pieces of tooling hide 18½in by 5½in

Water-bound white paste

Waxed linen thread

Piece of stiff card 4½in by 8in

Small quantity of plaster of Paris

Method

Choose the most attractive end of one of the pieces of leather for the front of the cover, measure in ½in from the sides and from one end and lightly mark with a pencil a centre panel 8in by 4½in, rounding off the corners. Mark this panel also on the flesh side for correct placing of the card stiffener later on. Choose your design and border to fill the panel. I used a daisy pattern punch for the border, then based the central design on this, making the basic daisy shape larger and slightly more elaborate. Trace your chosen design on the panel, then carefully dampen the leather all over with a moist sponge and draw around the traced outlines with a fid or other modelling tool. Take care not to get the leather too wet, and press hard enough with the fid for the lines to be seen faintly on the other side. Turn the leather over and, working on the flesh side, support the leather in the palm

Measurements of inner section of tooled hide notepad cover

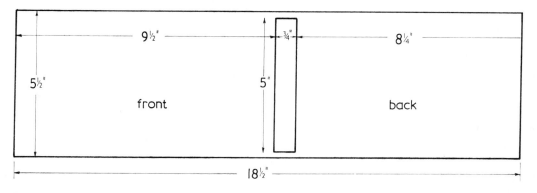

of your hand and press the areas you wish to appear raised on the right side. Be sure to keep the leather damp but not wet, and press evenly from the flesh side with a modelling tool. Turn back to the right side and add the smaller details with the fid to complete the design. Lay the cover on the work surface and imprint a border pattern around the central design with a decorative punch and mallet. This border pattern should be just inside the line of the drawn rectangle. Using a ruler and bone folder, draw another rectangle inside the first one to enclose the border pattern, rounding the corners to correspond with those already drawn. Mix up a little plaster of Paris and fill the hollows on the flesh side to prevent damage to the motif during use. Then trim the corners of the card rectangle to correspond with the corners of the drawn panel and paste the card to the flesh side of the panel. Place the cover, right side up, on the working surface and, using the fid, press the leather down around the edges of the card so that the decorative panel becomes raised above the surrounding area. Lay this section of the cover flat overnight to dry out. Meanwhile trim out the area to take the spiral part of the pad from the other rectangle of leather as shown in the diagram. When the outer cover is completely dry, paste the front part of the inner cover as far as the cut-out section, then paste the very edges of the back part of this section, leaving the centre part unpasted (the cardboard back of the notepad slides down inside the back of the cover for easy renewal). Paste the outer cover to correspond, then press both sections together and leave to dry thoroughly. Trim all outer edges level, using a ruler and a sharp knife, then round all four corners to correspond with the rounded corners of the decorative panel. Using a bone folder and ruler, score a line about $\frac{1}{8}$in from the trimmed edges all around on the right side of the cover. Mark stitch positions in this line with a No 8 pricking iron. Pierce the stitch holes with an awl and saddle-stitch around the edges with waxed thread. Burnish all cut edges, polish all over with a good colourless wax polish and buff to a shine. Trim the front cover from the notepad and place the pad in position by sliding the cardboard back down between the layers of leather at the back of the cover until the spiral wire settles into the cut-out area.

Blotter/writing case

71

No sewing is required to make this blotter. The pieces are cut to shape and assembled as shown in the diagram. The edges, however, must be skived neatly, so practise first on offcuts until you are quite sure you have mastered this skill thoroughly.

Materials
One large skin of dark green morocco
Two pieces of stiff card 15in by 10½in
Two pieces of stiff card 10½in by 7¾in
Two pieces of ¼in-thick plastic foam 10½in by 9in
Water-bound white paste
Latex adhesive
Contact adhesive
About 2ft of 1in-wide cotton tape

Method
Make a paper pattern of the large overall shape as shown by the dark shaded area of the diagram. Also make two rectangular patterns 10½in by 10in, two 10½in by 1in, one 10½in by 3in, one 10in by 3in and a right-angled triangle with the right-angled sides each measuring 4in. Examine the skin for flaws and marks, then lay the patterns on it and cut out all shapes with a sharp knife (edges will show in the finished work so they must be clean cut). Paste one side of each of the smaller pieces of card, then stick one 10½in by 10in piece of leather flesh side down on to each, with three edges meeting flush and the fourth edge extending about 2¼in beyond

Measurements of blotter/ writing case

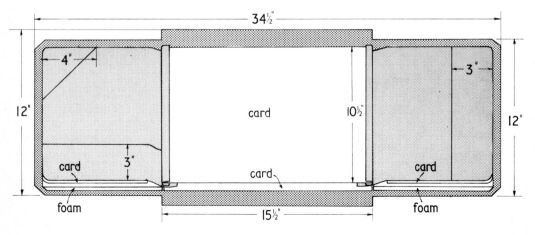

the edge of the card. Working on the flesh side, carefully skive the two short edges and one long edge of the 10in by 3in piece and the 10½in by 3in piece until the skived edges are paper thin. Set a screw creaser at about ⅛in between the blades, heat it and crease the right side of the unskived edge of each piece. Skive the flesh side of the two right-angled edges of the triangle and screw-crease the right side of the diagonal edge. Arrange these three shapes on the ready assembled card and leather rectangles as shown, with all the outer edges meeting flush. Stick in place sparingly around the edges with contact adhesive. Take the two 10½in by 1in strips of leather and skive the flesh side of one long edge of each, then screw-crease the right side of the opposite edge. Fold each strip in half lengthwise and stick one to each short edge of one of the largest pieces of card with creased edges to the right side of the card (this is simply to bind the cut edge of the card neatly). Place this bound piece of card face down on the work surface and arrange the ready assembled side pieces of the blotter face down on either side of it. The surplus leather part of each should overlap the bound edges of the card by about 1¼in. Stick these firmly in place with contact adhesive. Check that the skived edges are really smooth and tapered where they meet the card and, if not, trim off a little more. Then spread the other piece of card with a thin film of latex adhesive and centre it over the first piece pressing it firmly in place all over. Leave it to dry under a flat heavy weight for some time. Trim the edges level all around where necessary and round off the corners, or cut them to an oblique angle if preferred.

Using latex adhesive, stick one piece of foam to the card side of each outer cover, then mask the edges where the foam meets the card with tape, equally spaced over the join and stuck in place sparingly with latex adhesive. Leave this to dry thoroughly before proceeding. Latex adhesive takes a little longer to dry on plastic foam than it does on leather and card. Meanwhile, skive the flesh-side edges of the side parts of the outer cover, leaving the centre, top and bottom protrusions unskived. Centre the assembled inner part of the blotter on to the flesh side of the large leather shape. Stick the centre card section to the leather, but not the foam-covered part. When the centre section is firmly stuck, wrap the edges of the leather up and over the edges of the card and foam sections (allowing for ease when closing the blotter). Stick the centre part of the cover to the card at the very outside edges only, allowing the edge of the leather to remain free in order to slip the blotting paper under when it is finished. Stick the edges of the leather around the sides and ends of the blotter using contact adhesive very sparingly. This is quite a tricky job, and it is best to work on a small area at a time, keeping the cut edge perfectly straight and mitring the corners. When the adhesive has thoroughly dried, crease all cut edges with a heated screw creaser to make a decorative line, then polish all leather parts with a good clear wax, buffing to a shine. Cut several sheets of blotting paper 14½in by 9½in and slide them up under the top and bottom edges of the centre panel binding. Close the blotter and leave it for a few days with a weight on it to crease the fold lines firmly.

HIDE BELT WITH TWO BUCKLES

The ends of this belt have been divided and are fastened with two buckles instead of the conventional one. This makes an interesting focal point to an otherwise rather plain belt.

Materials
Strip of hide 2in wide and 10in longer than the waist measurement
Brown stain
2 buckles ¾in wide
Contact adhesive
Waxed thread

Method
Cut one end of the leather to the shape shown in diagram 1, rounding off the ends of the two straps and the area

Measurements of hide belt with two buckles

1

2

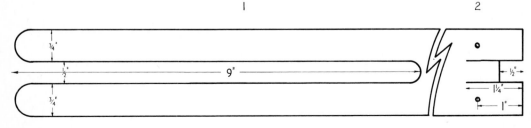

between them. Using a bone folder and a ruler, draw a line $\frac{1}{8}$in from the edge of the leather all around, rounding the curves to correspond with the cut edges. Damp the belt thoroughly all over but do not get it too wet. Then, using a decorative punch and hammer or mallet, imprint a pattern down the centres of the shaped straps and continue this pattern in a straight line down the body of the belt. Leave the belt to dry thoroughly, preferably overnight, and then stain it with the colour of your choice, following the hints on p59. Trim the opposite end of the belt, as shown in diagram 2, and skive the cut ends. Punch a hole in each of these short straps, 1in from the end, slide the buckles on to the straps, fold excess leather over to the back of the belt and stick in place with contact adhesive. Punch holes at 2in intervals in the shaped ends of the straps. Carefully stain the small offcut from between these end straps and punch a matching decorative pattern down the centre. Then wrap this strip around the belt about $3\frac{1}{2}$in from the buckle end and stick in place on the wrong side with contact adhesive. When this has thoroughly dried, stitch through the centre, making about three stitches to anchor it in place. This makes a neat 'keep' for the ends of the straps during wear. Polish the belt all over with a good quality wax polish and buff to a rich shine.

HIDE BELT WITH REPOUSSÉ AND PUNCHED DECORATION

Here is a very simple item to make which will enable you to experiment with relief decoration. One side of the meandering line has been raised with a modelling tool, whilst the other side is decorated with a punched all-over pattern.

Materials
Strip of hide 2in wide and 10in longer than the waist measurement
2in-wide decorative buckle
Contact adhesive
Coloured stain

Method
Trim off one end of the leather to a rounded shape, then dampen the strip evenly all over. Using a bone folder and a ruler mark a line down the long sides and the

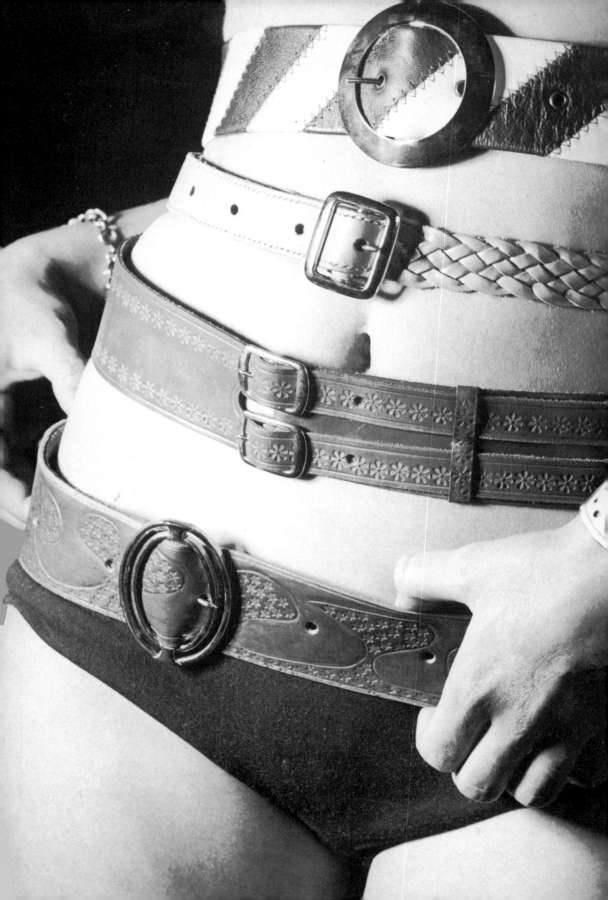

rounded end, $\frac{1}{8}$in from the edge. Using a modelling tool, draw a meandering line down the entire belt as shown in the photograph; then, working on the flesh side and taking care to keep the leather damp but not wet, push down the area between this line and the ruled line on one side to make a raised area on the grain side. Turn back to the right side of the belt and redraw the line where necessary to emphasise it. Using a decorative punch and hammer or mallet, strike a pattern on the unraised side of the belt, Leave it to dry thoroughly, preferably overnight, then stain it the desired colour (see notes on staining on p59). Punch seven holes at 2in intervals from the rounded end of the belt, then make another one 1in from the other end. Thread the buckle on to this end, passing the prong through the punched hole. Fold down the 1in surplus behind the buckle and stick it to the belt with contact adhesive. Polish the belt with a good quality wax polish and buff to a rich shine.

PLAITED HIDE BELT

This belt looks quite complicated but it is really very easy to make. Plaiting with four strands is no more difficult than using three, and the dampened leather is very pliable and easy to manage.

Materials
$1\frac{1}{2}$in-wide strip of natural hide 2in longer than the waist measurement
Strip of natural hide 5in by $1\frac{1}{8}$in
Two strips of natural hide each 10in by $1\frac{1}{8}$in
Contact adhesive
Waxed linen thread
Purchased buckle $1\frac{1}{4}$in wide

Method
Starting $\frac{1}{2}$in from one end of the largest strip of leather, cut it into six $\frac{1}{4}$in-wide strands (1). Thoroughly wet these strands by immersing them in warm water for a few seconds, then hang them up until they stop dripping but are still very wet. Clamp the uncut part in a vice, or pin it to the workbench with small nails or tacks so that it is firmly anchored and ready for you to start the plaiting. Begin to plait the strands, starting with the centre two and adding the others one by one (2, 3, 4). Keep the

A selection of leather belts: brown and white (p138), plaited hide (p77), double buckle (p74), repoussé decoration

grain side of the leather facing you all the time, bending each strand around in a curve at the outside edge to reverse direction (4). Keep the tension even and smooth and continue plaiting in this way to the other end of the strands. Clamp the loose ends of the plait together with a

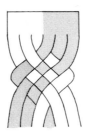

4

Method of plaiting and neatening the ends of a hide belt

1

5

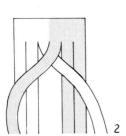

2

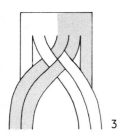

3

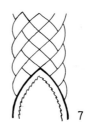

6

7

bulldog clip or a clothes-peg and then lay the plait out on the work surface grain side upwards and work over it carefully, flattening any bumps and making sure it is straight and even throughout. Leave it to dry thoroughly, preferably overnight. Meanwhile, cut both ends of each of the three other strips of leather into curved points (5). Carefully skive one end of one of the long strips and one end of the short strip on the flesh side. When the plait is thoroughly dry, trim one end (6) and using contact adhesive, stick in position to the skived end of one of the longest plain strips with the flesh sides together. Leave it to dry thoroughly. Trim the other plaited end in the same way and stick to the skived part of the short strip with flesh sides together. When the adhesive has thoroughly dried, carefully skive the ends of the plait within the area that is stuck to the plain strips. Using contact adhesive, stick the unskived long strip, with flesh sides together, to the other strip of the same length sandwiching the skived end of the plait between the two layers. Using a bone folder and a ruler, mark a groove about ⅛in from the edges all around the plain strip on the right side; then using a No 8 pricking iron and following this groove, mark stitch holes all around. Pierce the holes with an awl and saddle-stitch all round using waxed thread and harness needles. Trim the edges of the strip if necessary and burnish them; then punch a centre line of six holes about 1½in apart on the plain strip, using a punch which will make a hole to fit comfortably the prong of the buckle. Punch one hole in the very centre of the short plain strip, then with the bone folder and ruler mark a groove around the edges from the hole to the pointed end, leaving the half which is already stuck to the belt unmarked. Use the pricking iron to mark the stitch holes along this groove. Slip the buckle on to this end of the belt, so that the prong goes through the central hole. Fold the remainder of the strip back towards the belt and stick it in place over the skived ends of the plait. Pierce the holes with an awl and saddle-stitch around the edges where marked. To finish the belt, burnish the edge with a damp cloth then, using a soft brush, apply clear wax polish to the entire right side of the belt, buffing with a soft cloth to a rich shine.

Watch straps can be as simple or as complicated as you choose to make them depending on the style of the watch and the type of leather you choose. The most important thing about the design of a watch strap is that it should be comfortable to wear and have no sharp edges which will irritate the wrist. Buckles should be chosen to complement the style of the watch and should be easy to fasten and unfasten.

Generally speaking, the length of the finished strap including the watch should be about 2in longer than your wrist measurement, and if you plan to make a strap with a wide central area this should not be longer than half the finished length of the strap or you may have difficulty fastening the buckle. The width of most straps will depend on the width of the watch 'lugs' and you should choose a buckle which is as near this measurement as possible. Usually a small leather loop or 'keep' should be provided at the buckle end to keep the free end of the strap neatly in place.

Water-bound adhesive can be used where the strap is to be reinforced with stitching, but on unstitched straps a non-soluble adhesive should be used. Where the buckle is attached the turning allowed should be skived until it is paper thin at the very end, then turned through the buckle and stuck firmly down to make the inside of the strap as smooth and flat as possible. The ends of the leather keep should be sandwiched between these two layers before they are stuck. If you are using a stain, test it to make sure that it will not rub off on to the skin during wear.

Here is a brief description of the method of making the three illustrated watch straps.

Simple strap

The simplest strap is merely a long strip of leather which passes through the lugs and behind the watch. The strip was cut out 3in longer than the wrist measurement and as wide as the lugs of the watch; one end of this was shaped into a point and then a screw-creaser was used to mark a line around the edges. A small hole was punched 1in from the buckle end, then this end was carefully skived and trimmed. A short strip of leather was cut to make the keep and this was stuck in place about ¾in from the

Selection of simple watch straps

punched buckle hole. The buckle was then threaded on to the strap and the skived end was stuck down over the ends of the keep with contact adhesive. Five small holes were punched in the other end of the strap which was threaded through the lugs of the watch.

Double-sided Stiched strap

Two strips of leather were used for this strap, one for each end. They were both carefully skived down each long edge to give them a 'padded' look in the centre, then each one was threaded through the watch lug and stuck back to back with paste and finally top-stitched all around the edges. The pointed end requires no other fitting instructions, but the buckle end was worked as follows.

Punch a hole about 1in from the end of the strap. Do not skive or trim this end but make a keep and attach it in the same way as for the simple strap and then thread the buckle on to the strap and stick down the unskived end to cover the ends of the keep. Thread the other end of the strap through the watch lug until it is exactly the right length, then trim off the end, paste and stick the remainder of the strap firmly in place. Crease a line all around each strap and saddle-stitch.

Shaped strap

This heavy-duty strap is made from a piece of natural hide which has been tooled and stained and the watch is attached by two small shaped tabs, stitched on to the central area.

To make a strap like this, cut out two tabs to a preferred shape making one end narrow enough to pass through the lug of the watch and fold back on itself. If you like, tool a simple design on each tab, then stitch-mark them around the edges. Cut out the main strap to your own requirements – the one shown here has a central panel $4\frac{1}{2}$in by $1\frac{1}{2}$in and the remaining strap is $\frac{3}{4}$in wide. Tool it as desired, or simply crease the edges, then stain this and the two tabs, burnish the edges and leave to dry. Remember to stain some thread for stitching the tabs in place. When the stain is dry, skive the narrow ends of the tabs, thread one on to each watch lug and stick the skived ends firmly in place to the backs of the tabs. When the adhesive is dry, stick the tabs in place to the main strap, then pierce stitch holes and saddle-stitch

Shoulder bag with adjustable strap

in place using the stained thread. Attach the buckle in exactly the same way as for the simple strap.

(NB If you use a double buckle as shown on this strap you will not need a leather keep.)

TAN CALF SHOULDER BAG

This bag is made from one main piece of leather with side gussets to give it depth and shape. The shoulder strap fastens on with a buckle at either side of the bag and can be adjusted in length. A buckle and strap are used also for the front fastening and there is a flat pocket in the back of the lining to take a mirror. (One square in the diagram represents 2in.)

Materials

Piece of calf leather at least 45in by 12in
Piece of matching skiver at least 24in by 18in
Piece of buckram or other suitable stiffening at least 38in by 8¼in
Water-bound white paste adhesive
Three 1in-wide buckles
Stain to match the calf leather
Contcat adhesive
Linen sewing thread

Method

From the calf cut out a main rectangle 29¼in by 9½in, a shoulder strap 45in by 2in, two side gussets each 9½in by 3½in, two straps 3½in by 2in, one 4in by 2in and one 6½in by 2in. From the skiver cut out a rectangle 24in by

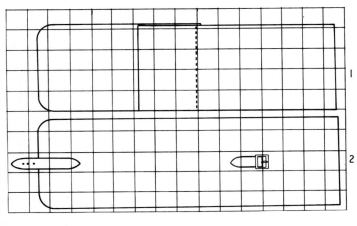

Pattern for shoulder bag and lining. One square represents 4sq in

$8\frac{1}{2}$in, another $15\frac{1}{2}$in by $8\frac{1}{2}$in and two more $8\frac{1}{2}$in by $2\frac{1}{2}$in. From buckram cut out a rectangle $15\frac{1}{4}$in by $8\frac{1}{4}$in and one $18\frac{1}{4}$in by $8\frac{1}{4}$in. Round off two corners at one end of the main rectangle of leather and two corners at one end of each of the leather gussets. Also round off the two corners of one $8\frac{1}{4}$in edge of the $15\frac{1}{4}$in long piece of buckram.

Make up the lining first in the following way. Take the $18\frac{1}{4}$in-long piece of buckram and paste it to the 24in-long piece of skiver, with the short edges level at one end and $\frac{1}{8}$in of skiver extending at each side of the buckram. Fold the skiver over the buckram and stick it to the other side so that the buckram is covered entirely on one side and partly on the other by the skiver (this partly covered side will form the inside of the pocket). Paste the other large piece of skiver extending $\frac{1}{8}$in beyond the buckram all around. Trim the corners of the skiver around the two curved corners of the buckram so that they extend $\frac{1}{8}$in beyond the edges. Leave both sections of lining to dry under a flat weight and then assemble them as shown in diagram (making sure that the overall length of the skiver, including the $\frac{1}{8}$in extensions, is exactly $28\frac{1}{4}$in). Stitch the two lining sections across the base of the pocket, as indicated in the diagram, stitching through both layers of buckram; then stick the skiver extensions together at the sides.

Skive all four edges of the main part of the bag and both the gussets to a depth of $\frac{1}{2}$in on the flesh side all around. Then turn in a $\frac{3}{8}$in hem all around each piece, carefully curving the rounded corners into small pleats and sticking all hems firmly in place. Paste the main lining and buckram section to the main bag section and leave heavily weighted until the adhesive has dried thoroughly. Trim two corners of each of the gusset linings to correspond with the rounded corners of the gussets and stick the lining in place to the gussets, leaving to dry under a weight.

Meanwhile, make the straps by folding all the strips sides to middle down their length and sticking them firmly in place. Attach a buckle to one end of both the $3\frac{1}{2}$in-long straps and to the 4in-long one, allowing a $\frac{1}{2}$in turning at the buckle end and skiving and trimming this to fit neatly to the wrong side of the strap. Stick this overlap firmly in place with contact adhesive. Trim both ends of the shoulder strap and the $6\frac{1}{2}$in-long strap, plus the opposite end of each of the buckle straps, into spear-shaped points with a sharp knife and then carefully stain the exposed edges of the leather with matching stain and burnish them. Draw a line, using a bone folder and ruler, ⅛in from the edge around all these straps on the right side, then mark out stitches with a No 8 pricking iron. When the gussets are thoroughly dry, position one of the two matching buckle straps on to the right side of each one with the centre of the buckle coming to within 1½in of the end without rounded corners and the pointed end of the strap extending down the centre of the gusset. Stick the straps in place to the gussets with contact adhesive, then pierce the stitch holes and saddle-stitch firmly in position.

When the main section of the bag has dried, rule a line around the edges and stitch-mark as for the straps, then place the remaining buckle strap on to the front part of the bag, as shown in diagram 2. Stick with contact adhesive, then saddle-stitch in place. Using contact adhesive very sparingly, and tying the sections together with thread (as described on p35), stick the gussets into the sides of the bag, starting at the front, keeping both sides level and even and easing the rounded corners of the gussets carefully into the lower corners of the bag. When these sections are all firmly stuck and tied together, saddle-stitch them in place, continuing to stitch around the front edges of the bag to secure the lining firmly at the edges. Position the double-ended short strap centrally on to the front flap of the bag, as shown in the diagram, and stick in place sparingly with contact adhesive, then carefully saddle-stitch in position all around. Saddle-stitch all around the edges of the shoulder strap, then punch suitably sized and spaced holes in both ends of this and in the free end of the front strap. Buckle the shoulder strap on to the sides of the bag.

SMALL WEEKEND OR OVERNIGHT CASE WITH ZIP-FASTENERS

This case is made from chrome-tanned hide which is very hard wearing and resilient. It has a fabric lining with a pocket set into the lid to hold small articles. Quite a lot of time is needed to make this case, so do not attempt to make it if you are in a hurry, and remember that it needs almost a half hide of leather.

Weekend/overnight case

Materials
Cut-out leather shapes:
Two rectangles 20in by 13½in for sides
One strip 19in by 6in for base gusset
One strip 45in by 4½in for lower side zip gusset
One strip 45in by 2½in for upper side zip gusset
One strip 45in by 1½in for zip guard
One rectangle 6½in by 4in for top press-stud flap
One rectangle 6½in by 5½in for lower press-stud flap
Two strips 21in by 1½in for handles
Two strips 63½in by 1¼in (joined where necessary) for piping

Other Materials
Two 22in heavy duty zip-fasteners
Heavy duty linen or polyester thread
Latex adhesive
Contact adhesive
1yd of heavy gauge piping cord for handles
1yd of 48in-wide fabric for lining
Two 18½in by 12in rectangles of stiff card
One 17½in by 3in rectangle of stiff card
One 17½in by 1½in rectangle of stiff card
Two large press-studs

Method
Cut out all the shapes listed from the leather, taking care to see that corners are true right angles. Use the best-looking part of the leather for the two largest rectangles, as they will be the parts to show most, the base gusset being the part to show least. Skive a ½in seam allowance on the flesh side of one long edge of both the 45in by 4½in and the 45in by 2½in strips. Fold over this allowance and stick the hems in place with latex adhesive. Using contact adhesive, stick both the zip-fasteners to these strips, with the folded edges of the hems meeting in the centre of the teeth of the zips, and the slide parts of the closed zips meeting in the centre of each strip. Mark a line with a bone folder and ruler, ⅜in from the folded edge down each side of the zips, then use a No 5 pricking iron to mark the stitch positions along these two lines. Pierce the stitch holes with an awl, and saddle-stitch down the marked line on the widest strip of leather to hold the zip firmly in place. Skive a ½in hem on the flesh

88

side of the 45in by 1½in strip down one long edge, then skive a similar seam allowance on the grain side of the opposite edge. Using contact adhesive, stick this strip to the unstitched side of the zip-fasteners, with the skived grain edge to the zip tape and the opposite edge facing the stitched side of the zip. Saddle-stitch in place to the unstitched edge as already described, stitching through all layers to hold the zip and the zip guard firmly in place. Trim the short ends of all strips level and skive them on the flesh side to a ½in seam allowance. Skive a ½in seam allowance also on the flesh side of the short ends of the 19in by 6in strip, then with right sides together, stitch this in place to the ends of the zipped strip with ½in seams, using a No 5 pricking iron to mark the stitches. This makes the continuous gusset for the case. Fold this seam allowance away from the zipped part, stick down with latex adhesive, then top-stitch in place using a No 5 pricking iron to mark the stitch line ¼in inside the previous seam line on the right side of the gusset. Using a race, make a groove to half the thickness of the leather, ½in from the edge of the flesh side, all around both sides of this continuous gusset. Trim the corners of the two large rectangles of leather to a rounded shape using a 3in-diameter circle as a pattern, then cut a seam groove, ½in from the edge the same as for the gusset. Clip away the excess seam allowance at the corners as shown, and mark stitches in this groove using a No 5 pricking iron. Skive a ½in seam allowance on the flesh side of the

Clipping away excess seam allowance from corners

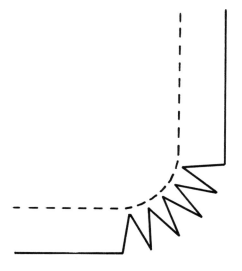

two small rectangles of leather, along two short and one long side of each, then trim the corners where the skived edges meet to a curve, using a 2in-diameter circle as a guide. Clip away the excess seam allowance at the corners and stick the seam allowance down with latex adhesive. Join the $1\frac{1}{4}$in-wide piping strips where necessary (as shown on p44) to make a $63\frac{1}{2}$in length for each side of the case; then join the ends of these strips to make two continuous bands. Spread the flesh side of these with a little latex adhesive, then fold them in half down the centres to make narrow piping (see p43). Fold the large rectangles to find the centre point of each side and mark these with a pencil. Find the centre point of the unzipped part of the gusset and mark this on each side, then find and mark the exact opposite point, and points midway between the marks already made.

To Assemble the Case

Place one piping strip along the right side of each edge of the zipped gusset, with the folded edge of the piping facing in towards the zip and the raw edge of the piping $\frac{1}{4}$in inside the raw edge of the gusset. Using an awl, pierce holes at intervals within the seam allowance and tie the piping firmly to the gusset with thread. With right sides facing, position the gusset around the sides of one of the large rectangles, matching all the marked centre points, and tie firmly in place within the seam allowance as already described. Position the other rectangle on the other side of the gusset, taking care to see that the zip-fasteners are slightly opened, so that you can get your hand inside the case. Tie in place as described. Find the centre point of the unhemmed edge of each of the small rectangles and place these, with their centre points matched and the right sides of the small rectangles facing the right side of the large rectangles. The larger one goes to the wide side of the gusset and the smaller one to the narrow side. Tie firmly in place. When all the sections are assembled, use an awl to pierce the marked stitch holes and then saddle-stitch all around each side of the gusset with strong waxed thread. When both seams have been stitched, open the zip-fasteners and turn the case to the right side, carefully easing out the corners. Remove all the threads used for tying the case together, then open out the seams and stick them down to the flesh side with latex adhesive. Ease all the corners and seams so that you get a smooth outline on the right side of the case.

To Make the Handles

Cut an 18in length of piping cord for each handle and stick this in place down the centre of each 21in by 1½in strip with latex adhesive, fraying the ends and sticking them as flat as possible. Cut the ends of the strips to spear-shaped points as shown on p49 (6), and mark a double stitch line around them using a No 5 pricking iron. Lightly coat the piping cord and flesh side of the straight part of the handle with adhesive, then fold in half down the centre to enclose the piping cord and press the edges firmly together p49. Starting 3½in from the spear-pointed end of each strap, mark a stitch line about ¼in from the raw edge and stitch both layers together down this line with strong waxed thread. Position the handles at the sides of the press-stud flap and tie firmly in position; then saddle-stitch in place with strong waxed thread.

To Make the Lining

Cut a strip of fabric 46in by 5in and stick this to the wide side of the case gusset so that one edge comes to the inner edge of the zip-guard seam allowance. Stick this seam allowance down over the raw edge of the lining to cover it. Cut another strip of fabric 46in by 3½in and press down a ¼in hem along one long edge with an iron. Using latex adhesive, stick this to the opposite side of the zip gusset, so that the fold comes to within ⅛in of the zip teeth. Smooth these fabric strips out and away from the zips, sticking them in place with latex adhesive used very

Turning end of lining over end of card stiffener for base

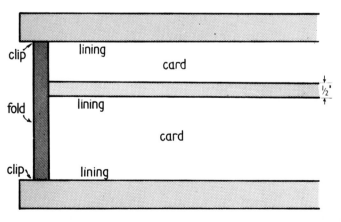

sparingly, and mitring the corners where the fabric falls around the corners of the case. Cut out an $18\frac{1}{2}$in by 7in piece of fabric and centre the two $17\frac{1}{2}$in long narrow rectangles of card on to the wrong side of this, so that there is a $\frac{1}{2}$in gap between them. Stick the card in place sparingly with latex adhesive. Clip into the seam allowance at the ends of the card as shown, and stick the seam allowance over on to the wrong side of the card with latex adhesive. When this has dried, coat the unzipped part of the gusset and also the back of the card sections with latex adhesive and place the lined card in the base of the case so that the gap between the card pieces corresponds with the line of the zip teeth. Press down firmly and leave to dry thoroughly. Stick the remaining seam allowances of the lining smoothly down to the sides of the case, mitring the corners where necessary. Cut out two $20\frac{1}{2}$in by 14in pieces of fabric and one 12in by 8in. Turn under a $\frac{1}{2}$in double hem along one long edge of this smaller piece and machine-stitch in place, then turn under a $\frac{1}{2}$in single hem around the other three sides, mitring the corners. Position this small piece of fabric on to the centre of the right side of one of the larger pieces to make a pocket, and stitch in place around the three unstitched sides. Trim the corners of the two $18\frac{1}{2}$in by 12in pieces of card to a rounded shape, using a 3in-diameter circle as a pattern. Centre a piece of card on the wrong side of each large fabric rectangle and stick in place sparingly with latex adhesive. Turn the edges of the fabric over on to the wrong side of the card, mitring the corners and sticking firmly in place with latex adhesive. Coat the inside of the sides of the case with latex adhesive and also the wrong side of the lined card rectangles; then press these firmly in place, with the pocketed panel in the lid part of the case and the plain rectangle in the base. Using a press-stud tool, fix a press-stud to each corner of the flaps between the handles, so that they overlap to make a handy place for carrying a rolled umbrella or newspaper. To make opening and closing of the zips easier, thread a small piece of leather through the opening in the zip slide to act as a pull tab.

Part 2
Dressmaking with Leather and Suede

If you are used to dressmaking, you should have no difficulty in making garments from leather provided you follow a few basic rules which are common sense more than anything else.

In the following pages I have described the procedures for choosing leathers and making up leather garments. I have assumed that the reader has a basic knowledge of dressmaking techniques and terminology and is used to making garments from the more usual fabrics. If you are not too confident in your skill it might be well worthwhile to take an evening-class course in dressmaking; then, under the watchful eye of a trained instructor, you can brush up your knowledge and practise the many different techniques.

Your first garment in leather should be very simple – a plain skirt or a short waistcoat or something which takes only a couple of skins. Then it will not prove too costly should you make a mistake. Once you get the feel of the material, you can go on to something more complicated. All leathers have their own particular character, but this is something you can really get to know about only first-hand.

Most clothing leathers are made from sheepskin, but you can also get calf and split hide. Joining the comparatively small areas that can be cut from a sheep skin accounts for the panelling and seaming in most garments made from this kind of leather. A split hide garment will have fewer seams.

When choosing both leathers and patterns, think about wear and cleaning. Remember that suede tends to get soiled fairly quickly so it is often worth paying a little extra for a washable one, and worth choosing a washable lining also. Most of these skins are supplied with printed instructions on how to clean them.

All the garments shown in this book were made either on an old treadle sewing machine or on an ordinary swing-needle electric one, so no special equipment is needed other than that used for normal dressmaking.

Although leather is not cheap to buy you will find that the garments you make will be about half or three-quarters the price of those sold ready-made, and you will have the added advantage of perfect fit, plus the choice of co-ordinating colours and styles to fit in with your existing wardrobe. Never throw away the offcuts unless they are really tiny. Store them in a box or bag to use up in patchwork, or to make small toys and other items which can be given away as birthday presents. Bags of offcuts can sometimes be bought from manufacturers of clothing and it is often worthwhile looking for advertisements in magazines for these. Patchwork waistcoats and cushions can be made very cheaply and simply, particularly if you have a swing-needle sewing machine.

STYLES AND PATTERNS

For those who are not familiar with making their own patterns many of the proprietary purchased patterns can be adapted for use with suede and leather, provided they are of suitable design. Owing to the size of the individual skins of most clothing leathers, large, plain areas are usually impractical. Garments cut in panels are therefore the best designs to choose; gored skirts, trousers with a horizontal seam at the knee and jackets with a yoke and two-piece sleeves are usually the most suitable. Unless you are using a very thin and supple leather avoid patterns with full gathered sleeves or waists, as these tend to be rather lumpy and can be almost impossible to sew. Steer clear, too, of closely fitted garments which rely on a lot of darts for their fit. On the

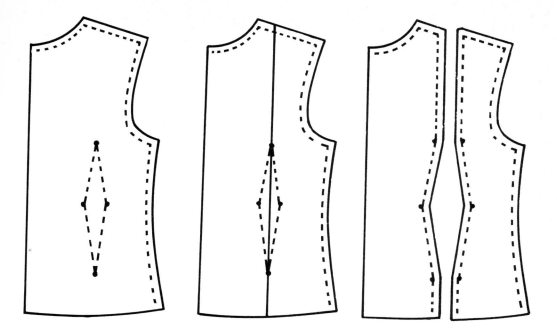

Turning a dart into a seam

whole, seams tend to lie flatter than darts, and so in some patterns darts can be turned into seams by extending them and adding seam allowances as shown. This also helps to avoid waste in cutting out, since two small shapes can more easily be fitted on to an awkwardly shaped skin than one large complicated shape. Comfort should also be borne in mind when choosing your pattern; remember that leather and suede tend to be thicker and stiffer than most fabrics so seams and darts in uncomfortable places should be avoided wherever possible.

To make sure of a perfect fit it is a very good idea to make up a pattern first in handicraft felt, as this type of material hangs in a similar way to leather. Cut out the shapes and tack them together, then try on and adjust the fit. You will find it well worth the extra time and expense involved because leather is not cheap and mistakes cannot always be rectified.

Well-made leather and suede clothes will last a long time so remember to buy good quality linings, threads and other items. It is as well also to choose the more classic styles rather than the current fashion fads which will date long before the garment has given good wear.

Since all leather is produced in skin form and cannot be bought by the yard like fabrics a different way of estimating the amount needed is required. As a very rough guide, a waistcoat will take two fairly large skins, one for the front and one for the back. A skirt will also take two large skins; a jacket with sleeves will probably need five or six skins, depending on the style and the size of the skins, and a similar amount will be needed for a pair of trousers.

Most leather and suede suppliers will send cuttings of the colours and qualities of the skins they sell and they will also tell you their approximate size. If you go along to a shop or store to buy your leather you can take your patterns with you, and then you will have no trouble in estimating the amount you need to buy. If you order by post it is better to over-estimate the amount you need; you can always use up the extra for something else such as a small toy or a patchwork cushion. Skins are tanned and dyed in batches so different batches tend to vary slightly in colour, as in the case of knitting yarns, and if you order too few you may not get exactly the same colour again.

The Right Type of Leather for the Garment

Colour is not the only thing you will have to choose when buying your leather. Thickness and texture are very important too, so think carefully about the type of garment you will be making, how much wear it will get, and how often it will need cleaning. Remember that grain leather will keep clean much longer than suede which, because of its surface texture, tends to get marked very quickly. Thus an outdoor coat or jacket would be more practical in grain leather whilst a waistcoat or other smaller garment could be made from suede. When it comes to cleaning most firms charge according to the size and type of garment and this is worthwhile bearing in mind when choosing your materials. Some washable suedes can now be obtained in a really beautiful range of colours; these are soft and supple and can be used for blouses and dresses.

At this point I must include a warning – never use chamois leathers (as manufactured for cleaning cars, etc) for garments which will be worn next to the skin. I have seen quite attractive garments made from this material but the chemicals used in the processing of wash leathers are less refined than those used for clothing leathers and can cause allergies and nasty skin complaints.

Plan your cutting layout and arrange all your patterns before starting to cut out. Where a pattern shape indicates that it is to be placed on a fold, cut out the shape from folded paper to use as a pattern; never fold the leather and try to cut it double since it will move and the shape will be inaccurate. You will not have to worry about fabric grain lines, so small shapes can be dovetailed in with larger ones to avoid waste. Most clothing leathers are machined to make them a fairly uniform thickness all over, the thicker parts being shaved away. There will, however, be slight variations in the thickness so pay attention to this when arranging your patterns. Remember that seams are made up of two, three or even more thicknesses, and when you are using a sewing machine there is a limit to the amount with which it will happily cope. Areas like collars, which are stitched and then turned and top-stitched, should be cut from the thinner, side areas of the skin.

Some people prefer to cut out from the wrong side of the skin, after examining the right side carefully for flaws and marks which must be avoided. If you work this way you can attach your patterns to the wrong side of the skin with adhesive tape before cutting out. I find its safer to lay the patterns on to the right side, weight them down with something flat and fairly heavy and then draw around the shapes with chalk and remove the patterns before cutting out the shapes. It is much easier this way to see what the skin is like in the areas you are cutting and thus avoid any holes or marks.

Ordinary dressmaker's scissors can be used, provided they are good and sharp, but a ruler and craft knife or leather knife will be much quicker and more accurate for long straight lines. Sharp creases can be removed by ironing the leather or suede on the wrong side with a medium hot iron and a dry cloth. Never use a damp cloth or the leather could become marked and hardened in patches. When all the shapes have been cut out they should be laid flat until ready for sewing to avoid creasing them again. It is not a good idea to iron leather or suede repeatedly but it can be done occasionally without damage.

Since all pin and needle holes would permanently mark the skin, tailor's tacks cannot be made to indicate pattern markings. The relevant marks should instead be transferred to the wrong side of each shape with chalk or a pencil. Notches in seams can be clipped out and hem allowances on facings and similar pieces can be trimmed away since the leather will not fray and turnings like this will only add extra bulk to show through the garment as unsightly ridges and bumps.

LININGS

Linings should be chosen for colour, comfort and durability. Also bear in mind washability if the leather or suede used is a washable one. I have found that some cotton and cotton/wool lightweight mixtures make rather good linings as well as the synthetics made specially for lining fabric. Choose your lining with care and remember that the more expensive ones usually last longer than the cheaper ones. Make up the lining as directed on the pattern instructions. A garment such as a suede waistcoat will not need to be lined, because the smooth side of the leather will be on the inside. A similar garment made from grain leather, however, will need lining to prevent small particles of leather from rubbing off from the flesh side and spoiling any other garment worn underneath.

INTERFACINGS

Most good tailoring and dressmaking interfacings can be used for leather with the exception of some of the iron-on varieties. It is not generally a good idea to use this type of interfacing for several reasons. The first point is that owing to the moisture in it being removed, leather shrinks quite considerably during ironing, but it goes back to its original size quite quickly once the heat is removed and, if an interfacing has been fused on to it in the meantime, it will tend to wrinkle because it cannot stretch back into shape. The second point is that the adhesive used for some interfacings is not dry-cleanable, and once the garment has been dry-cleaned the interfacing comes away from the leather, which then becomes limp and floppy.

For collars and other areas which need to be really firm, hair canvas is suitable. This can be obtained in various weights to suit the job in hand, so select one which is the right weight for the garment and the leather you are using. In some areas where interfacing is called for in a fabric garment, it can be omitted from a leather one because the leather is perhaps firmer in texture than fabric would be. Conversely, where fabric garments rely on their weave to take stress in a certain direction, some fine leathers may be interfaced with a very fine fabric, such as lawn, to prevent them from stretching out of shape.

To avoid bulky seams and hems, trim off hem and seam allowances from the interfacings and stick them in position on to the wrong side of the leather with an adhesive, used very sparingly, and mainly around the edges. Thereafter treat as one fabric. For belts, buckram can be used since it is really stiff and will keep its shape well.

Make sure that any tape, seam binding or similar sewing notion is pre-shrunk or shrink resistant before using. This is most important for washable garments like the evening skirt on p127 which relies on tape for its assembly.

ADHESIVES

Seams can be stuck flat and hems turned up by using adhesive, but first decide whether the garment will be dry-cleaned or washed as this will affect the type of adhesive employed. For garments which will be washed a latex adhesive such as Copydex can be used, but this is soluble in dry-cleaning fluids so it can only be used as a temporary measure during the making up of the garment, which must then be top-stitched to hold the seam or hem permanently in place. Where top-stitching in this way would not enhance the garment, seams and hems can be stuck in place with an adhesive such as Bostik Clear which is insoluble in both water and dry-cleaning fluids.

THREADS AND TRIMMINGS

Good silk or linen thread is the best kind to use. Silk thread is obtainable in a whole spectrum of colours, whilst linen is usually supplied in the natural shades of beige, brown and grey. The gauge of thread will depend on the thickness of leather you are sewing and, for fairly heavy jobs, silk buttonhole twist is ideal. For hand-stitching and hand-stitched buttonholes, it is a good idea to wax the thread first, both for added strength during wear and also to help it to slide through the leather when sewing. Bound buttonholes can be made very successfully on leather and for jackets and coats they look most professional.

For some garments craft leatherworkers' tools can be used; for example, eyelet punches for belts, and press-stud tools to attach press-studs. Zip-fasteners are very useful, particularly the open-ended cardigan type, but choose sufficiently strong ones since it is much easier to put a zip into a garment when making it up than it is to replace a broken one later on. Whether you choose metal or nylon zips is a matter of personal choice, but recently there have been some attractive heavy-duty plastic ones available in some stores, and these are decorative as well as functional. Buckles and buttons are also chosen because of their decorative aspect as well as their usefulness, but don't go mad! The appearance of many a good garment has been spoiled by the wrong choice of buttons.

STITCHING

By Hand

All stitching must be accurate from the start. Unpicked seams will always show as a row of little holes, so great care must be taken with every dart and seam. Hand-sewing in leather is not difficult if the right type of needle is used. A glover's needle is most useful; it is triangular in section and the angles are sharpened into extremely sharp blades near the point to enable it to cut through the leather easily. Glover's needles are made in different sizes for various types of leather, but the most useful size for a wide variety of jobs is size 3. When sewing with a glover's needle, wax the thread and stitch the seam with close, evenly spaced stab-stitches. For added strength, instead of finishing off at the end of the seam, unthread the needle and replace it with a blunt-pointed harness needle. Retrace the stitches, going through the holes made by the glover's needle but in the opposite direction, so that you end up with a continuous line of stitching on both sides of the seam. It is most important to use a harness needle for this second part, since the sharp blades of the glover's needle would cut through the stitches already made.

With a Sewing Machine

As previously mentioned I have used two sewing machines for the garments in this book – a modern electric one with attachments for embroidery, button-holes and all the other new refinements, and an old treadle probably made about the year 1900, which is built like a tank. The old treadle is generally much more sympathetic to working with leather. It will take thick layers without a murmur, whilst the modern one will just chew them up. For the thinner leathers, however, the modern one is ideal, especially if I want to use a zig-zag stitch for a particular effect. It is not necessary, therefore, to have an up-to-date and expensive sewing machine although it is helpful for certain jobs. The main thing is to get the needle, thread, tension and pressure of the foot correctly adjusted, and to be patient always and try out on an offcut first. Some sewing machine shops sell special needles for sewing leather. These are spear pointed and the edges of the spear shape are sharpened into blades so that they cut cleanly through the leather. They are very helpful with the thicker types of leather, but on the thinner ones they tend to make rather large holes and so an ordinary needle is best used here. For some makes of machine you can also get a special foot which has two small rollers to help the leather to roll smoothly under the needle. This type of foot is especially useful if you have the type of machine which does not have an adjustable pressure foot. On machines where you can vary the weight of the pressure foot it is usually adjusted by a knob or screw at the top of the machine directly above the pressure foot column. You will soon find out which way of turning reduces or increases the pressure. This should be set so that the leather is just held firmly enough under the foot to prevent you from pulling it out, but loose enough to allow the teeth to feed it through consistently.

You will probably find that silk thread is easier to use with the machine than linen thread, which seems to have a will of its own and unwinds madly, especially when you are trying to fill the bobbin. Stitch sizes should be varied to suit the thickness of the leather. For most clothing about eight to ten to the inch is about right. Avoid using stitches that are too small, as these could cause a weakness in the leather and lead to tearing along the stitch-lines. Sometimes you will find that the machine will miss a whole line of stitches, just leaving a long straight thread on both sides of the seam. This could be because the seam is too thick owing to some obstruction such as adhesive between the seams, or because the thickness is uneven at either side of the pressure foot. Provided the length of the unstitched part is not too long, the easiest way to deal with this is as follows. Thread a blunt harness needle with similar thread; then working from the wrong side go up through the holes made by the machine, one at a time, over the top thread and down through the same hole again. This catches down the top thread and looks the same as the rest of the line of stitching without breaking the original thread. When top-stitching grain leather, take care in inserting it under the foot of the machine, as the feed teeth can scratch and tear the surface of the underside.

PRESSING SEAMS

Instead of pressing seams open or flat with an iron as is usual for fabric garments, leather seams are hammered flat and stuck down, then sometimes top-stitched both for decoration and to keep them firmly and strongly in place. A hammer with a rounded face, like the one shown in the diagram, is the best type to use as it does not make

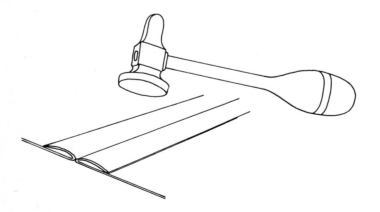

Using a round-faced hammer to flatten seams

sharp 'edge' marks. A rawhide hammer or mallet like those used by jewellers is also useful, since it is softer than a metal one and less likely to cause damage should you miss the target.

Some Problems You May Encounter

SETTING IN SLEEVES

Generally speaking, two-piece sleeves fit into the armhole much smoother than one-piece sleeves, so choose this type whenever possible. Sometimes, however, you will choose a pattern with one-piece sleeves and these may need slight adjustment before cutting out. As already mentioned it is wise to make up the garment in felt first– in this case to see whether the sleeve head needs altering. Remember that it is more difficult to ease leather than it is to ease fabric; you cannot shrink a leather sleeve into an armhole as you would be able to shrink a wool fabric, for instance, so the excess fullness will have to be trimmed carefully away from the sleeve head. If you have done a lot of dressmaking you will be able to judge, by just looking at the shape, whether a sleeve head is likely to be too full and you can trim away the excess accordingly as shown without altering the length or the hang of the sleeve. If you are not so sure about this, try it out on the felt pattern until you get it quite right, then trim the leather to the same shape. For some one-piece sleeves it is easier to put them into the armhole before the side seams of both the bodice and the sleeve are stitched. Match the centre top of the sleeve head to the shoulder seam, then ease the sleeve in from this point down either

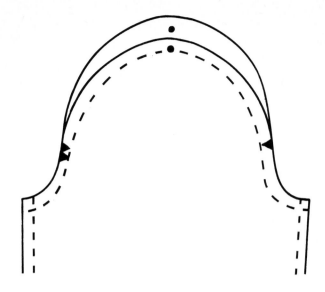

Trimming away excess full-ness from sleeve head

side. When you reach the underarm seam you can trim away the excess leather from the sleeve, provided it is not a very large amount; otherwise you could end up with a sleeve that is too tight. Always ease in as much of the fullness as you can, without making it look gathered.

Trimming away excess full-ness from sleeve

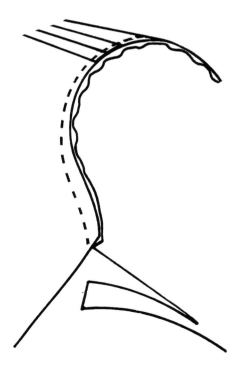

It oftens helps to clip into the seam allowance around the armhole. Clothes-pegs, bulldog clips and Sellotape can be used to hold layers together, and then the sleeve should be stab-stitched in place within the seam allowance,

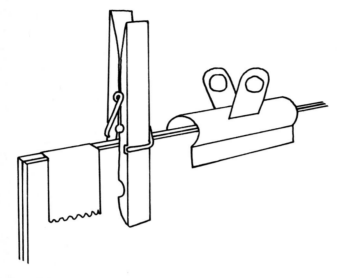

Adhesive tape, clothes-peg and bulldog clip holding two layers together

using fairly small stitches to hold the fullness firmly in position. Stitch close to the line of stab-stitching taking care to prevent any puckers or small pleats from forming in the sleeve head as you sew. Most fabric garments have the seam allowance around the sleeve head pressed towards the sleeve, and this can be done with leather

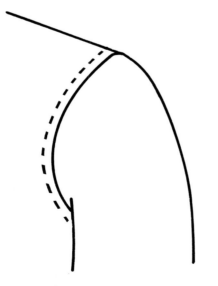

A turned and top-stitched seam

also. Sometimes, however, if the leather is fairly thick, the seam may not lie flat on its own. In this case it can be trimmed, turned towards the bodice of the garment and stuck, then top-stitched all around like a shirt shoulder to keep it firmly in place.

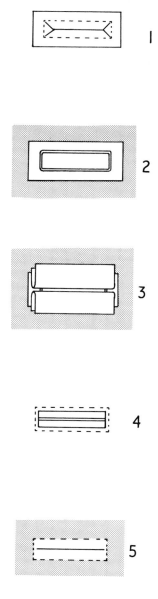

A hand-stitched bound buttonhole

BUTTONHOLES

Hand-stitched buttonholes are fairly simple to sew on leather if you use a suitable needle. For thin, supple leathers ordinary sharps are suitable provided they have a good keen point. With these you can stitch a fairly close line of buttonhole stitches, but take care not to get them too close together or you will cause a weakness in the leather which could tear with continuous use. For heavier, tougher leathers use a glover's needle in the smallest size you can easily thread with buttonhole thread. Space the stitches evenly to avoid shearing through those already made with your sharp-bladed needle. Use a buttonhole twist and wax it before sewing to help draw it through the leather. To prevent distortion of some thinner leathers and to give the buttonhole added strength, a piece of pre-shrunk tape can be inserted between the main pattern and the facing before stitching. This will stop the leather from stretching out of shape or tearing during use. If you glue this in place, use the adhesive very sparingly or it may be difficult to sew through.

Bound buttonholes give a really professional finish to jackets and coats as well as to many smaller garments. These are quite easy to adapt to leather and suede. I find that it is best to use a fairly thin matching colour fabric or a pre-shrunk tape for the first stage. Stitch this in place on the right side of the leather; then clip the centre (1) and turn the tape or fabric through to the wrong side. Pull it out flat and hammer down well all over and then stick firmly in place (2), making sure you cannot see it easily from the right side of the buttonhole. It is usually a good idea to make up the first stage of bound buttonholes before you start to make up the front of the jacket or whatever the garment happens to be. This avoids wrestling with a large section of leather which could get damaged whilst you are continually turning it around to stitch the buttonholes. Add the lips to the buttonhole (3), sticking them firmly in place on the wrong side with adhesive. Choose thinner leather for this part. If the garment is in suede, these sections can be made from the grain side for longer wear and an attractive contrast effect. The half-finished buttonhole can be left at this stage until the jacket is more or less finished; then, when the facing is stitched in position and turned to the inside, simply stitch through all thicknesses around the buttonhole from the right side (4). On the facing side simply cut a slit between the stitched lines (5).

PREVENTING STRETCH ON SEAMS

When seaming together two layers of suede or leather, you will frequently find that the top layer stretches under the foot of the sewing machine and if you are not careful you end up with a curved or frilly seam. This can be prevented to some extent by slackening off the tension of the pressure foot, but this may not remove the problem entirely. The best method I have found of preventing this is to stick a length of pre-shrunk tape along the seam line of the top layer (1) and to stitch through this. The tape will not stretch as you sew and will hold the leather firmly in shape. Where you are stitching curved seams, clip into the inner curve (2), then ease the two sections together and stitch them; finally, open seams flat (3). Always stitch seams from top to bottom, then if they do stretch a little despite all your care you can trim off the excess from the hem allowance. If you stitch from bottom to top and are left with uneven ends you may have difficulty

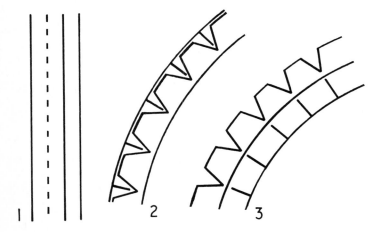

Preventing stretch on seams

in fitting them accurately to other pattern sections. The problem of the top layer stretching and puckering when you are top-stitching an edge can be prevented by sticking the two layers together inside with adhesive before starting to stitch.

ADAPTING COLLAR PATTERNS

Many collars for fabric garments are cut from folded fabric and the pattern instructions say 'place on fold'. This is not practical for leather, so you must make a pattern from folded paper, open this out and use it to cut out your leather. Collars cut out in one piece like this tend to be rather large, so be extra careful when placing them on the leather. Make sure that one end is not

Some collars

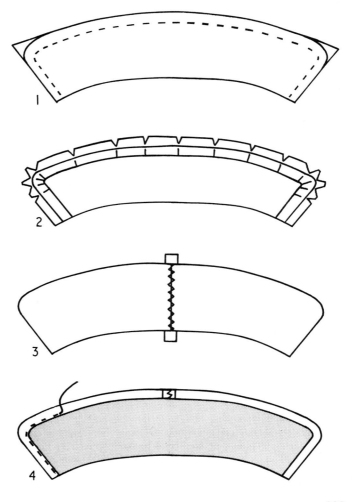

positioned on a thick part while the other end is on a thin part of the skin. This would show when the collar was made up, since one end would be stiffer and firmer than the other and might react differently to top-stitching.

Turning collars the right way out after they have been stitched can be quite a problem. For this reason avoid sharp-pointed lapels and corners; round them off (1) and they will be much easier to turn. To assist in turning them, the surplus leather can be trimmed neatly away from the edges (2), and the seam allowance clipped out at intervals in small, wedge-shaped pieces. The turnings can then be folded down and stuck in place to the main part of the collar on both sides before turning. This also helps to prevent any puckering caused by the top layer creeping on the bottom layer during top-stitching around a collar. Do not trim away too much of the seam allowance, however, since this may make an unbalanced ridge to stitch over and, if the pressure foot of the machine has to straddle an unequal thickness, it may not stitch properly. In order to prevent this, allow at least the width of the pressure foot to remain where the edges are to be top-stitched.

In order to avoid extra bulk where the centre seam of the undercollar occurs (unless, of course, you have enough leather to cut this in one piece), trim off the seam allowance and butt the centre edges of the undercollar together over a piece of tape. Stick in place and then zigzag-stitch them together (3). Where you are stiffening the collar with an interfacing, trim off the seam allowances from this and stick it to the wrong side of the undercollar with adhesive used sparingly, mainly around the edges. Stitch the upper and under collars together in the normal way, just outside the edge of the interfacing (4). The surplus leather will then turn over easily and fold flat. Turn out the ends of the collars carefully with the blunt end of a pencil or the handle of a spoon. Do not push too hard or you may burst the stitches or tear the leather.

PREVENTING BULKY SEAMS

In cases where seams cross over one another or meet, you may find that this area, on the wrong side, becomes bulky with seam allowances which need to be trimmed away for a smoother fit. For example, if you are joining a vertically panelled lower bodice to a yoke, the seam allowance at the

110

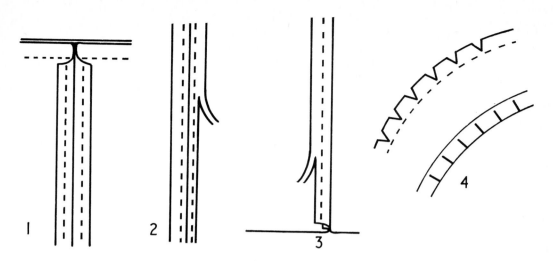

Trimming bulky seams

top of the vertical seam can be clipped neatly away before stitching it in place to the yoke (1). If this is done carefully it will result in a much more comfortable seam on the inside and a smoother, neater appearance on the outside. Where you are top-stitching a seam in a garment the excess leather can either be trimmed away from the seam afterwards (2), or, if the seam allowance is folded to one side only and then top-stitched, the inner layer can be trimmed away inside the seam first and then the outer layer trimmed close to the stitching-line afterwards (3). The seam allowance from curved seams (4) should be clipped out in small wedge-shaped pieces to enable the seam to be stuck or stitched down flat. Edges and corners can also be skived in the same way that you would skive a wallet or a bag (see the craft section p33), using a sharp knife or razor blade. Take care, though, not to cut through the stitches when doing this as it may be very difficult to restitch a skived seam satisfactorily.

POCKETS

Patch pockets are ideal for leather and suede garments. With top-stitched edges they add a decorative touch as well as being functional. They can be lined or left unlined, depending on the garment and the type of leather. If you intend to line your patch pockets there are two basic ways to go about it. The first is to cut out from lining fabric the pocket shape minus the seam and hem allowances and stick this carefully in place to the wrong side of the pocket, placing the adhesive around the edges only of the lining.

111

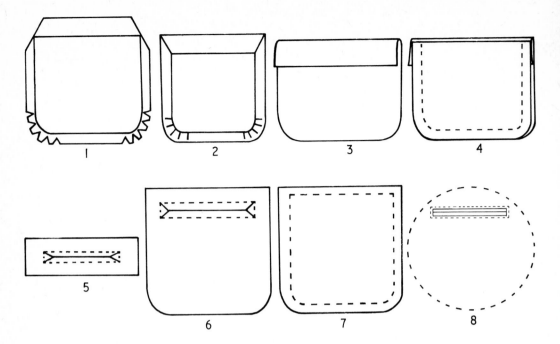

Clip into the curves and mitre the corners around the hem allowance of the leather pocket shape, then turn this over and stick into place on the lining (1, 2).

The second way of lining this type of pocket is to cut out the whole shape, including seam allowances, from the lining fabric. Fold down the top of the leather pocket to the right side (3), place the lining over this and stitch the edges together round the sides and base (4), and then carefully turn right side out through the opening at the top of the lining. On both these methods top-stitch the top hem of the pocket in place before stitching the pocket to the garment.

Unlined pockets can be turned in and stuck without the lining (2), or they can be left with raw edges, depending on the type of garment you are making and the firmness of the leather.

Pockets in the seams are a little more tricky to make than similar fabric ones as the leather will usually need to be reinforced around the area of the pocket-opening to prevent it from stretching out of shape during wear. Apart from this, these pockets should be made according to the particular pattern instructions.

The easiest way to make inset pockets where there is no seam is to do them rather like bound buttonholes. First of all, paste a piece of thin but firm fabric on the wrong side of the garment where the pocket slit will be placed (5), then position one of the pocket shapes on the garment with right sides facing, and slit marking corresponding, and stitch around the pocket slit (6). Cut the slit and turn the pocket through this to the inside of the garment. If desired, make lips for the opening the same way as for bound buttonholes (see p107). If not, simply top-stitch around the pocket slit to strengthen it and to give a decorative finish. Place the other pocket shape in place over the attached pocket with right sides inside and stitch the two together around the edges (7).

For an unusual style pocket on a sporty jacket or on a pair of trousers, follow the first three stages of the bound buttonhole on p107, top-stitch around the opening and, after trimming away excess fabric and leather from the wrong side, simply place a circle of leather behind this and stitch around it, working from the right side of the garment to give a neat line of stitching. You will probably find it easier to stick the edges of the circle in place before stitching around. You will then have to feel through the right side of the garment for the edges of the circle and stitch about $\frac{1}{4}$in inside this line to make the pocket (8). This type of pocket does not, of course, have to be a circle—any fairly simple shape can be used, provided it is convenient as a pocket. You can, if you wish, insert a zip into the opening instead of lips.

WAISTBANDS

Since leather will stretch with movement during wear, it is best to make waistbands from a material which will hold its shape well. Petersham ribbon is probably the most well-known kind of waistband material and this is ideal for leather and suede. As well as preventing stretch, this kind of waistband will guard against the small suede particles which can rub off from the inside of the waist of a skirt or trousers and spoil the blouse or whatever you wear under it. Remember to make small pleats if the waistband is curved to allow for the widening of the garment towards the hips. Full details of attaching a petersham waistband are given in the evening skirt instructions on p130.

As leather and suede are expensive and often bulky, and as, in the case of suede, there is the problem of particles rubbing off or 'crocking', it is often more sensible to line small garments such as waistcoats edge-to-edge, thus doing away with bulky leather facings. This is the most simple way of lining a garment; you just make up the lining fabric in exactly the same way as the garment, but without pockets, belts, collars, etc, then stitch the two together around the outside edges. In the case of a waistcoat, it is best to leave the shoulder seams of both the garment and the lining unstitched until after the lining has been attached. Then turn the whole thing right way out, after clipping into curved seams of course, and stitch the shoulder seams of the leather by machine. Turn under the seam allowance at the shoulders of the lining and slip-stitch in place neatly over the leather shoulder seams. Finally, top-stitch around the neck, front, hem and armholes of the waistcoat to prevent the lining from rolling out under the edge of the leather during wear. This method is described, step-by-step, in the instructions for the patchwork waistcoat on p132.

Linings for skirts should be made in the same way as the

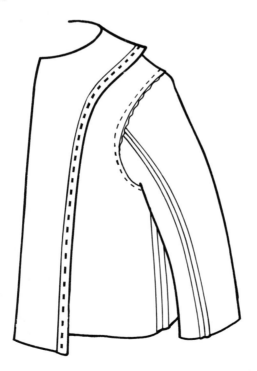

Jacket with bias binding stitched to edge of facing for attaching lining

main garment, then the leather and the lining skirts should be hemmed separately before the lining is attached. Make the lining about 2in shorter than the skirt to allow for a slight stretch during wear. When the lining is in place in the leather skirt the waistband can be attached through both layers as if they were one. Finally, slip-stitch the opening in the lining to the zip tape down each side of the zip.

Where facings cannot be omitted, as in the case of jackets or coats, the best way of attaching the lining is to bind the inner edge of the facing with bias binding as shown in the diagram. When the lining has been made up, it can be placed inside the jacket and slip-stitched to the bias binding by hand. This makes it easy to remove and replace should it wear or become torn. The sleeve hems can be bound in a similar way, and the lower hem of the lining bodice can be stitched separately and allowed to hang free of the jacket.

FASTENINGS

The type of press-studs which are punched in place rather than sewn make very useful and decorative fastenings. They are made in a large range of different sizes as well as some colours, nickel and brass. Decorative effects can also be made with eyelets, the larger sail eyelets and various shaped studs. All these items are now sold pre-packed in the haberdashery departments of some of the larger stores and come complete with a fixing tool and instructions on how to use them.

On some thin leathers it is necessary to reinforce the area around a press-stud, and this can be done by sticking a small piece of firm but thin fabric to the wrong side of the leather. Do not extend the adhesive to the very edge of the fabric or it may form a ridge which will show through to the right side of the leather. To reinforce buttons, sew another smaller button on the inside of the garment, stitching both the buttons and the leather with each stitch. If the main button is not a shank type, make a thread shank by sewing the buttons on loosely then winding thread around this between the main button and the leather to hold them apart. This will allow for the thickness of the buttonhole and make it easier to fasten and unfasten the button without puckering the area around the buttonhole.

Zip-fasteners are usually inserted in the normal way, but are first stuck in place with a suitable adhesive instead of being tacked. Zips in leather and suede garments often look best if the folded edges of the leather meet down the centre of the zip teeth except for some of the larger, more decorative zips which can be inserted with the teeth exposed. If you have trouble in opening or closing the zip, rub the teeth and the inside of the folded leather at each side of this with a little beeswax or tallow to make it run smoothly. Take care though not to get any wax on the surface of the suede as it could cause greasy marks.

HEMS

Unlike dressmaking with fabrics, leather and suede hems are almost never stitched by hand. Some people prefer to leave the edges of some of the firmer leathers unturned and not hemmed at all, but I personally feel that this can look unfinished unless you are making a garment with a fringed edge. Hems can be stuck firmly in place with a washable, dry-cleanable adhesive, or stuck and then top-stitched in place.

When sticking a hem, do not extend the adhesive to the very edge of the leather because this edge may show through the garment as a bulky ridge. Stick from the fold to within $\frac{1}{4}$in of the cut edge. Remember that this hem will be a permanent one so get the fold in the right place first time and then trim away any excess hem allowance—a $1\frac{1}{2}$in-2in-wide hem is plenty. Fullness cannot always be successfully eased into a leather hem, so clip out small wedge-shaped pieces until the fullness fits in perfectly, but never extend the cuts all the way to the fold or you will get little angular points all around the hem.

If you plan to top-stitch the hem in place, first stick it down as already described and then stitch around it on the right side. If you stitch from the wrong side the teeth of the machine may mark your hem and spoil it. Zigzag stitches can be used for a decorative effect, or ordinary straight stitching in single or multiple parallel lines.

TROUSERS

The secret of successful trouser making is to get a pattern which really fits well. If it does not, adjust it until it does.

If possible use a pattern which you have already made successfully in fabric so that you know how and where it will need adjustment before you start. Alternatively, make up the trousers in felt first, then adjust them before cutting the leather. Since you will not be able to get the whole length of the leg out of one skin (except for children's trousers), you will have to choose a pattern which has a horizontal seam just above the knee, but make sure that this is above the knee and not on it or the constant wear in bending and stretching will split the seam. You can adapt an ordinary trouser pattern by cutting it across and adding seam allowances to each cut edge. Lining will help to stop the trousers from becoming baggy at the seat and at the knee, but choose a good strong fabric for this because it will be taking all the strain in these areas. There is no need for the horizontal knee seam in the lining; in fact it is better cut in one piece since the seam might show through the leather as an untidy ridge. Join the lining to the trousers at the waist and zip opening only, to avoid any pulling and puckering elsewhere, and hem them separately.

The procedure of making leather trousers is the same as for fabric ones. You can have flat plain seams, top-stitched flat seams, or you can turn the seams to one side and top-stitch them for extra strength and decoration. A waistband can be made from petersham ribbon as described on p113, or if the trousers are to be worn over a blouse with the waistband showing, it can be cut from the leather. In this instance, in order to take the strain and stop the waist from stretching out of shape, insert a piece of wide tape or a strip of strong fabric inside the band before stitching. Zips can be incorporated into fly fronts or inserted at the side, depending on the pattern instructions. Try to avoid unnecessary bulk wherever possible, especially at the waist, by trimming seams or paring them away inside with a craft knife. With some very thin leathers belt loops can be added, also made from the leather, but this is not possible on thick leathers because they would be too difficult to attach through all the thicknesses.

Hems of trousers must be judged accurately, then stuck and top-stitched in place. Remember to wear the shoes you will wear with them as even a small heel will make a lot of difference to the finished length and there is nothing worse than trousers which are just too short. When you have made one pair successfully you can experiment with such fashion ideas as buttoned flys, laced flys, fringing, bib and brace tops and turn-ups.

FRINGING

Many garments can be fringed around the hems for decoration and this is a very easy, if rather time-consuming, way of finishing off. Decide how long you want the fringe to be and adjust the pattern accordingly, then when the item is made up the fringe can be cut. Trim away the seam allowances from the vertical seams to the depth you want the fringe to be; then cut the hem allowance into vertical strips with very sharp scissors. It is always best to rule a line inside the garment where the top of the fringe will end, then you will be sure of getting a nice even top edge to your fringe. For wildwest-type jackets a fringe can be inserted into the back seam of a two-piece sleeve in the following way. Decide how long you want the fringe to be, then add a seam allowance to this to correspond with the seam allowance on the jacket. Cut a strip of leather to this width and as long as the sleeve seam from the armhole to the turned edge of the cuff. Insert one edge of the fringe strip between the two sleeve pieces when you stitch the back seam; then, when the sleeve is made up, you can cut the strip into a fringe. It is always best to leave the cutting of fringes until the last when making up a garment as otherwise they tend to get tangled or perhaps inadvertently stitched into seams, etc. Fringes can be added to hems, cuffs, the lower edges of yokes, the outside seam of trouser legs, the base of pockets and many other places to add interest to otherwise plain garments.

Hand-sewn Gloves

Glove making is really a separate craft in its own right, but I am including it here because gloves are usually made from leather and suede.

Making your own gloves is a very rewarding and relaxing pastime. Hand-made leather and suede gloves work out much cheaper and better than purchased ones and, of course, you can choose colours and styles to suit your wardrobe. No special tools are required and all the materials and equipment can be kept in a large chocolate box.

Purchased patterns are used, and the ones most generally available are the F.A. Staite patterns. These can be bought from shops and stores which sell other kinds of dressmaking and knitting patterns. Staite patterns are supplied in $\frac{1}{4}$-sizes 6 to $7\frac{1}{2}$ for women and in $\frac{1}{2}$-sizes $7\frac{1}{2}$ to 9 for men. They tend to be rather long-fingered and slightly larger than purchased gloves of the same size number.

A glove pattern consists firstly of the main part, called the trank, which has fingers and a thumb hole; secondly a thumb; and thirdly a finger gusset called a fourchette. Some patterns also contain a small diamond-shaped gusset for the base of the finger called a quirk which is used in conjunction with a special double fourchette. It

119

is advisable for beginners to start by using single four-chettes, without quirks.

Patterns can be altered slightly in length but not in width. To ascertain whether the finger length will need altering, slip the pattern on to the hand with the thumb going through the thumb hole, then see whether the distance between the base of the thumb and the base of the first finger is too long on the pattern. If so, move the thumb hole up a little when you cut out your leather. When this distance has been altered, you can trim off the tips of the fingers if they are still too long. The tip of the thumb can be trimmed off in a similar way. Never try to widen the fingers of the main pattern. If they are too tight, widen the fourchettes instead. Remember that firm leather which does not stretch so easily will make up into a smaller glove than a more stretchy one, and to give extra ease across the hand on firm leathers $\frac{1}{8}$in can be added to each side of the palm. Extra length can be added to the hem of the glove, and gauntlet gloves can be adapted by inserting a wedge-shaped gusset in the base of the side seam to allow the glove to fit over a coat cuff.

Leather and suede used for gloves must be supple and not too thick. It is best for beginners to start with a fairly firm textured leather which will be easier to stitch than the stretchy ones. You can then graduate to the finer, more expensive skins made especially for gloves when your stitching has become perfect. Gloving needles are used only for the thicker, tougher leathers as they would make rather large unsightly holes in really fine skins. For these, ordinary sharp or between needles are used, in the smallest size that will take the thickness of the thread through its eye. No other equipment is needed other than a good, sharp pair of scissors, strong thread to match the leather (silk buttonhole twist is very good) and some wire paperclips to hold the sections in place whilst you sew.

The skins sold for glove making are usually sufficient for two pairs of gloves and it is possible sometimes to buy half a skin only. Such skins are usually divided in half across the back, not down it, and patterns are always placed with the stretch of the leather running across the hand from side to side for ease during wear.

For each hand you will need to cut out one trank, one thumb and six fourchettes, three of these reversed left to right in order to make three pairs. Patterns are usually

Underarm folio (p66) and hand-sewn gloves

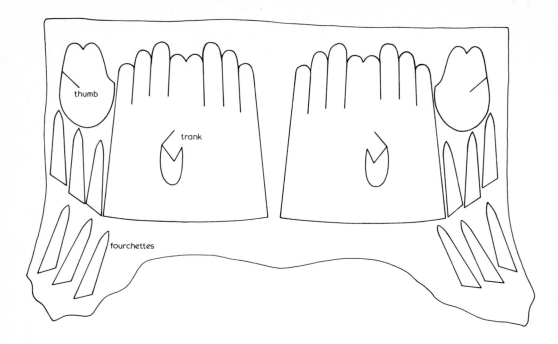

laid out as shown in the diagram, the backs of the hands being arranged next to each other on the best looking part of the skin. Make sure that both backs match up well in colour and texture because these show most during wear. Take care also to avoid any hardness or thickness in the very centre back of the skin where the animal's backbone was, as this will not stretch easily during wear. Arrange the fourchettes and the thumb at the side of the skin in the thinner part of the leather and see that the stretch runs across these from side to side. At the upper and lower corners of the skin, where the animal's legs were, the stretch tends to be slightly diagonal, so plan your cutting layout accordingly.

Lay the pattern on the right side of the skin and mark around it carefully with a bone folder or a pencil. Never use a ballpoint or felt-tip pen. Reverse the pattern shapes for the other hand, then cut out all the shapes with very sharp scissors. Remember that the cut edges will all be on the right side of the finished gloves, so any uneven or badly cut edges will clearly show.

All the pattern pieces are assembled in the following way. Take the thumb and match up points A and B on the thumb and the thumb hole. At this point, the thumb will be positioned upside down on the main part of the glove

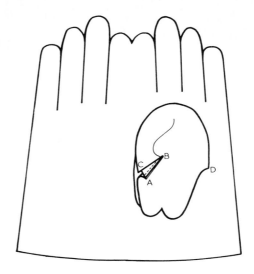

The first stage of stitching the thumb into the thumb-hole

as shown. Start stitching them together at point A, using the type of stitch you prefer, stitch to point B, then to point C and continue to about halfway down the front of the thumb hole. Fold the thumb in half so that the curved parts at the top are matching and, starting at the fold, stitch down to point D, then down and around the base of the thumb to where you left off before. Take care to see that the base of the thumb fits smoothly into the thumb hole without gathering or puckering. If the hole seems too small stretch it carefully around the base until the thumb fits perfectly.

The next stage is to stitch the points, the three tiny tucks down the back of the hand, and then hem the glove if this is necessary. At this stage add any applied decoration to the back of the hand or the cuff. You are now ready to join the fingers. Join a pair of fourchettes at the base, with the right sides facing, and start stitching on the wrong side at the shortest side of the fourchettes ending at the point of the base with about 8in of thread left over. Take this hanging thread through the base of the back of the first finger and stitch the fourchette to this finger to about half way. Measure the fourchette against the finger and trim off the surplus, then reshape the fourchette to a point and continue to stitch it up to the top of the finger. Stitch the back of the second fourchette to the second finger in the same way, then join the other pairs of fourchettes and stitch them to the backs of the other fingers similarly. Fold the glove in

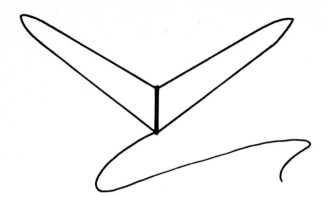

half down the centre, and thread the needle with a long piece of thread. Starting at the folded edge of the top of the first finger, stitch the fourchettes in place to the front of the hand, stitching down one finger and up the next in a continuous seam and taking care to see that the base of each pair of fourchettes fits tidily down between the fingers. Continue stitching over the top of the fourth finger and down the side of the glove to close it.

There are several types of stitch which can be used for sewing gloves. The easiest of these is a simple stab-stitch which looks just like a running-stitch but, unlike the latter, you only pierce through the leather in one direction at a time. Simple oversewing can be used but this must be kept very neat and even or it tends to look rather untidy. Buttonhole-stitch and blanket-stitch are both very popular because they give a neat, firm edge to the glove seams. Another stitch which also gives this firm edge is whip-stitch, sometimes called double oversewing, because the needle passes twice through each hole for extra strength.

The threads for sewing in the thumb and the backs of the fourchettes should be kept very short so as to prevent them from getting tangled with the fingers of the glove while you are sewing. All the stitching is started with a knot which can be hidden carefully inside the seams. The stitch tension should be kept firm and even but never pulled too tightly. Remember that it is the strength of the thread and its tension which prevents a glove from stretching out of shape, particularly if you are using very fine and stretchy leathers, so pay particular attention to this.

Decoration

Gloves can be adorned and decorated in a variety of ways, the cuffs and backs being the best part to decorate since this will not interfere with the construction of the glove. Unusual stitches can be used for the points, or these can be sewn with contrast thread. Different-coloured leathers can be appliquéd on to the gloves; they can be laced or thonged, punched with different-sized holes, or have patterns painted on them with suede dyes.

When your gloves are finished, fold the thumb of each in towards the hand, flatten the fingers by tucking the fourchettes into pleats within the fingers, then wrap each glove in some tissue paper, place it in a magazine and weight it down with a pile of books for a few days to press it into shape.

Some Garments and Accessories to Make

SUEDE EVENING SKIRT

Here is a very attractive and unusual evening skirt made from washable suede. The diagonal chevron stripes have been planned so that no really large pieces need to be cut out. You can, therefore, arrange all the shapes on the suede with a minimal amount of wastage. This skirt took a total of five large skins (about $6\frac{3}{4}$ to 7sq ft each) plus lining fabric, tape and thread.

Materials
3 large skins of washable suede in main colour
Matching silk sewing-thread
1 skin dark contrast washable suede
1 skin light contrast washable suede
About 34yd $\frac{3}{4}$in-wide preshrunk tape
Latex adhesive
An 8in matching zip-fastener
3yd 36in-wide washable lining fabric
1yd $1\frac{1}{4}$in-wide petersham waistband

To Make the Pattern
Measure around your waist and divide by four and call this measurement 1. Wearing the shoes you will eventually wear to give the correct height, measure from your waist

Washable suede evening skirt with matching patchwork waistcoat and evening bag

to the ground and call this measurement 2. Following diagram 1, make two paper patterns from these measurements and put one aside to use for the lining later on. Fold the other pattern in half down the exact centre, then measure and mark off the diagonal stripes (2), lettering them as you go for easy identification. Place the folded pattern on a cutting board and, through both thicknesses, cut out the stripes with a sharp knife. (Cutting through both layers together makes sure the chevron will fit accurately at both ends.) Letter the stripes from the other side of the folded pattern, then divide all sections in half down the centre fold.

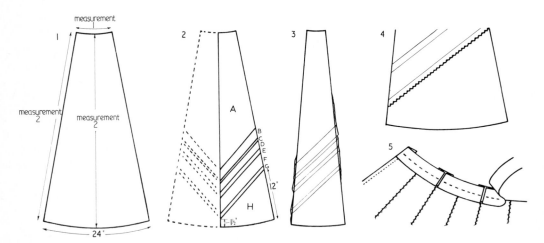

To Cut Out

Lay out the three main colour skins and cut out four of each left and right side of shapes A, D and H from these, dovetailing the pattern pieces on the skins with the least wastage, and drawing around them all before cutting any out to make sure they will all fit. Accurate cutting of all straight lines is essential on these shapes as lines which are not quite straight can cause unsightly puckering in the skirt when they are assembled. Keep the cut-out shapes in their piles of four so as not to get them mixed up. Now cut out four of each shape B, E and G from one contrast colour, and four of each shape C and F from the other contrast colour. Lay out all the shapes in piles of four in the order they will eventually be assembled.

Making an evening skirt. Width of stripes: B, 3in; C, $\frac{1}{2}$in; D, $1\frac{1}{2}$in; E, 1in; F, 4in; G, 1in

To Assemble

Clear a large working surface and cut off seven 15in lengths from the tape. Place one of these on the table and hold it firmly in place in a straight line (sellotaping the ends to the table is a good idea). Paste this tape all over with latex adhesive, then butt the top edge of one piece H and the lower edge of one piece G together down the centre of the tape, taking great care not to get any adhesive on the right side of the suede. Press the joined pieces down firmly along the seam line and leave to dry thoroughly. Then lift from the table, turn over and rub away any surplus adhesive from the wrong side. Paste another length of tape and butt the top edge of piece G to the lower edge of piece F in the same way. Repeat this procedure until one whole vertical section of the skirt is complete, remembering to remove any surplus adhesive from the wrong side as you go. Make up the other seven vertical panels in the same way, then, one by one and using a long ruler or other straight edge, mark the edges in a straight line down each side (3). Trim off any uneven edges so that all sections will fit smoothly together. Thread the sewing machine with the main colour thread and set it to a largish zigzag stitch. Top-stitch down all the butted seams to hold them firmly in position (4). Pull all ends of the threads through to the wrong side and knot them securely before trimming off the surplus. Cut off eight lengths of tape to fit the side seams of the panels, then anchor the tape, paste and butt the panels together in pairs in the same way as for the stripes, easing where necessary but avoiding too much stretching to prevent puckering of the skirt. Carefully remove any surplus adhesive from the wrong side of each double panel before stitching. Zigzag together as for the stripes, then join again in pairs. Finally join both large sections to make the whole skirt. Leave the top end of one seam open to the length of the zip-fastener. Stick the zip-fastener carefully in place with latex adhesive, taking care not to get any on the teeth of the zip, then machine-stitch in place with a line of straight stitches all round. Turn up a 1in hem around the base of the skirt and stick it in place with latex adhesive, then straight-stitch all round about $\frac{1}{2}$in from the folded edge. Using the pattern you set aside, but adding $\frac{1}{2}$in down each side for seam allowance, cut out four panels of lining fabric. Seam these together in the normal way, leaving an opening at the top of one seam for the zip opening of the skirt, and then press all the seams open. Turn up a 2in hem around the lower edge of the lining and stitch it in place. With wrong sides together, insert the lining into the skirt, matching the zip openings. With the top edges level, stick the lining to the top of the skirt with a little adhesive to hold it firmly in place whilst stitching. Cut a length of petersham 4in longer than your waist measurement, turn down ½in at each end and stick it neatly in place. Position the petersham waistband around the skirt, as shown in diagram 5, making a box pleat at the side of the skirt opposite the zip, plus one at the centre front and one at the centre back to take up the extra length of petersham. Stick sparingly in place with latex adhesive, then stitch in place all around close to the lower edge of the petersham. Turn the petersham down to the inside and slip-stitch in place to the lining, opening out the box pleats as necessary to allow for the widening of the skirt towards the hips. Stitch the lining fabric in place to the zip tapes at the opening.

PATCHWORK SUEDE WAISTCOAT

Here is one way of using up the smaller offcuts. This waistcoat is made from the small scraps left over from the evening skirt; they were cut into squares and stitched on to a thin fabric backing.

Materials
Scraps of different coloured suede
Thin, pre-shrunk fabric for backing (an old sheet is ideal)
Latex adhesive
Silk thread in one of the suede colours
About 1yd of 36in-wide lining fabric
Buttons, press-studs or frog fastenings

Method
Make paper patterns for all the shapes following the diagram (scale: one square represents 2in) and use to cut out two of each shape from the backing fabric. Tack these shapes together and try on to adjust for a perfect fit (this pattern can be adapted for bust sizes 35in to 38in but similar patterns can be bought in other sizes). When you are satisfied with the fit, cut out the lining fabric from the same pattern. Look carefully at your scraps of suede

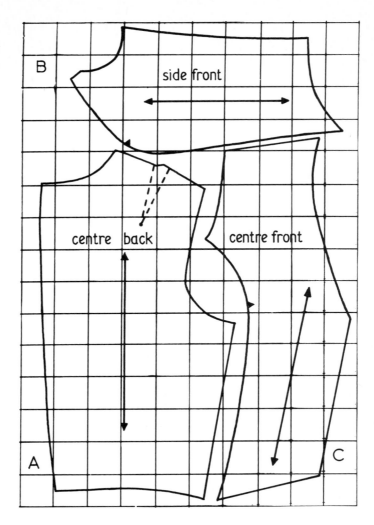

Pattern for a patchwork waistcoat. One square represents 4sq in

Labels within the pattern: B, side front, centre back, centre front, A, C

and decide on the size and shape of your patches. Diamonds or squares are the best shape because they have only four sides and can be stitched together in rows. Make a template and start cutting out the patches. You will find this rather a time-consuming and repetitive occupation, but it can be done while you are watching the television or during any spare moments of the day. You will need more patches than you think—the waistcoat shown here took about 375 squares of $1\frac{1}{2}$in each—so do not make your patches too small or you will be forever cutting them out. When you think you have enough mark out the right side of the backing fabric into corresponding shapes with a pencil; this will enable you to place all the patches accurately. Take care to see that the horizontal lines of the shapes are matched up wherever possible. Arrange the patches on to the backing fabric in a pleasing pattern of colours and stick them carefully in position with latex adhesive used very sparingly. When all the patches are firmly stuck on, stitch them in place down the joins in rows using a zigzag machine-stitch.

To Make Up the Waistcoat

First of all, stitch the shoulder darts on the two pieces A, then join these down the centre back with a $\frac{1}{2}$in seam. Clip into the seam where it is slightly curved, open it out and stick it down flat with latex adhesive. Join the two side fronts B to the centre fronts C with $\frac{1}{2}$in seams, clip into the seams, open them out and stick them flat, as already described. Join the back and the fronts together at the underarm seams, but leave the shoulder seam open. Make up the lining in exactly the same way, but press the seams open with a cool iron instead of sticking them down. With right sides facing, position the lining on to the suede section and stab-stitch in place all around the very edges with a glover's needle and thread, taking care to see that all seams in both lining and suede are matched up and lying quite flat. Now machine-stitch the two layers together around the neck edge, centre front, lower hem and armholes, leaving the shoulder seam unstitched. Trim the seam, clip into the curves where necessary, then turn the whole waistcoat right side out through one of the shoulder openings. With right sides facing, join the shoulder seams of the suede with $\frac{1}{2}$in seams, press the seams open and stick them down flat. Overlap the lining shoulder seams over this and slip-stitch to close them neatly. Working on the right side of the waistcoat, top-stitch all around the neck edge, centre front, lower hem and armholes about $\frac{1}{4}$in from the edge with matching thread.

Fastenings

Ordinary buttons and buttonholes can be used here, or press-studs. If you wish you can be more adventurous and choose frog fastenings or eyelets and laces. The type of fastening should depend on the style of skirt or trousers the waistcoat will be worn with.

Chevron evening bag to match washable evening skirt

This attractive bag is designed with the same sort of chevron stripes as the evening skirt so that it can be used with it. The frame was bought from the haberdashery department of a large store and then the bag was planned to fit round the size and shape of the frame. If you cannot get the frame size shown here you can adapt the pattern by scaling it up or down to fit another frame.

Materials

An evening bag frame 6½in by 2¼in (closed) with chain
    handle
Large offcuts of suede in three colours
Latex adhesive
Piece of lawn or other fine fabric 13in by 8in
Silk sewing thread to match suede
Piece of lining fabric about 24in by 8in
Contact adhesive

Method

Draw the pattern on to folded paper from the diagram (scale: one square represents 1sq in) and cut out only the main shapes from this. Do not divide into the chevron stripes yet. Use the large main pattern to cut out one shape from lawn and one shape from lining fabric, then use the small gusset shape to cut out two side gussets from the lining fabric. Divide the main pattern by cutting along the chevron stripes, then cut out the largest part from the main colour suede and the other two parts from the contrast colours; also cut out two gussets from the main colour suede. Arrange all the sections of the main striped part on the piece of lawn, butting the edges together, then stick them carefully into place with latex adhesive. When the adhesive has thoroughly dried, zigzag stitch the stripes together along all the joins. Trim the side edges level where necessary then, on the right side of the striped section, most carefully spread a little adhesive down the very edge of each side edge, extending the adhesive ⅛in in from the edge only. Very sparingly spread the adhesive down the sides and notched end of each gusset on the right side in the same way. Then leave all sections until the adhesive becomes transparent. When it has all dried, place right sides facing and join the edges of the gussets and the main part of the bag together down each side, matching notches

*Pattern for a chevron even-
ing bag*

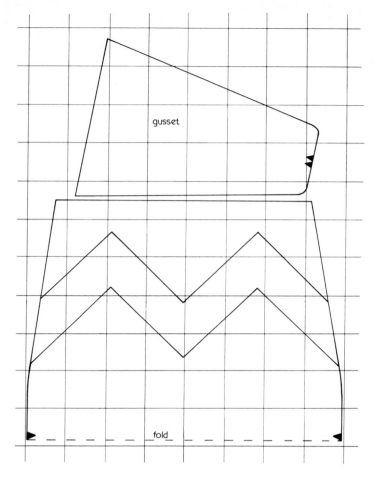

gusset

fold

and the top edges of each section. Press firmly into place,
easing around the lower corners where necessary; then
zigzag-stitch down each seam to hold the sections firmly in
position. Press the seam towards the main part of the bag
and stick carefully in place with latex adhesive (this will give
a crisp outline to the side edges of the bag). Turn the bag
right side out. With right sides facing, pin, tack and stitch
the lining sections together in the same way as for the bag,
matching the notches and top edges. Trim the top edges of
both bag and lining to make them level, then insert the lining into the bag with the wrong sides together. Stick the
lining carefully to the top of the bag, again using the latex
adhesive sparingly and round the very edges only. Open out
the frame and spread the contact adhesive, a little at a time,
around the inside edge; then press the top of the bag
firmly on to this, easing it right up inside the top edge of

135

the frame and paying special attention to the corners, particularly if they are a little bulky. The centre top of the gusset should come to the hinge of the frame sides and the side seams should fit neatly into the top corners of the frame. When the bag is firmly in place and the adhesive has dried, thread a needle and stitch the bag firmly in place through the small holes in the frame. You can use stab-stitching or oversewing, whichever you prefer, but it is best to use double thread for a strong join.

GOLD LEATHER EVENING BAG

Add a touch of glamour to your accessories with this pretty dorothy-style evening bag. It consists of only two main pattern pieces and can be made from some larger offcuts.

Materials
Rectangle of gold leather 16in by $7\frac{1}{2}$in
Circle of gold leather $5\frac{1}{2}$in in diameter
Strip of gold leather 22in by $\frac{3}{4}$in (joined where necessary)
Rectangle of lining fabric $16\frac{1}{2}$in by 5in
Circle of lining fabric 6in in diameter
Matching sewing thread
Circle of stiff card $4\frac{3}{4}$in in diameter
Latex adhesive
Ten large brass sail eyelets

Method
Fold the rectangle of leather in half with the right sides together and join the two short ends with a $\frac{1}{4}$in seam to make a continuous band. Open the seam out and stick down flat with latex adhesive. Insert the circle of leather into the base of this band with the right sides together and the edges level and stitch in place around the edges with a $\frac{1}{4}$in seam. Trim the seam and clip into the curve where necessary, then stick the card circle firmly to the circle of leather with latex adhesive, pulling the seam allowance clear of the sides of the card. Stick the seam allowance to the edges of the other side of the card so that the stitched seam lies smoothly along the edge of the card. Turn the bag to the right side. Make up the lining in the same way as the bag, but make $\frac{1}{2}$in seams instead of $\frac{1}{4}$in ones and press them out flat with an iron instead of sticking them down. With the wrong sides together, insert the lining into the bag, pushing down the base until it lies quite flat in the

Suede spectacle case (p158) and gold leather evening bag

OPEN AIR THEATRE

ASON

, N.W.1.

David Conville

-486 2431

bag. Stick $\frac{1}{4}$in of the top edge of the lining to the sides of
the bag, matching the side seams and keeping the lining
fitting smoothly to the lower sides and base of the bag.
Turn down $1\frac{1}{2}$in of the top of the bag to the inside to cover
the top edge of the lining and stick this in place with latex
adhesive. Leave to dry thoroughly. Mark the positions for
the ten sail eyelets around the top part of the bag. They
should be about $1\frac{1}{4}$in from the top and about $1\frac{1}{2}$in apart.
Insert the eyelets using an eyelet punch as instructed on
the pack.

To make up the drawstring, working on the wrong side
fold the narrow strip of leather sides-to-middle down the
entire length and stick firmly in place with latex adhesive.
Cut off the ends obliquely and fringe them. Starting at one
side of the seam, thread the drawstring alternately in and
out of the sail eyelets, then knot the ends with a reef knot,
leaving about $1\frac{1}{2}$in of the fringed ends hanging free for
decoration.

BROWN AND WHITE STRIPED BELT

Soft nappa leather was used to make this attractive belt of
alternating diagonal stripes. It was sewn on a swing-
needle sewing machine, but you can make it quite
successfully using an ordinary straight-stitch machine.

Materials
Largish offcuts of brown and white leather
Strip of calico 4in wide and about 45in long
Latex adhesive
Brown silk thread
A $1\frac{3}{4}$in-wide buckle with prong
Brown eyelets and eyelet punch
Contact adhesive

Method
Follow the diagram (scale: one square represents 1sq in)
to make paper patterns of both shapes, then use these
to cut out one large brown, thirteen small brown and
thirteen small white shapes from the leather. Iron the
strip of calico and lay out flat on the work surface, then,
using latex adhesive and butting all the long edges
together, stick all the leather shapes on to the calico
starting at one end with the largest brown shape and
alternating the colours of the smaller strips. Keep the

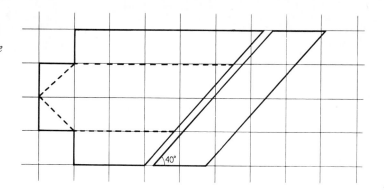

Pattern for a brown and white striped belt. One square represents 1sq in

short ends of all the strips level with the edge of the calico. When the adhesive is thoroughly dry, stitch down all the butted joins using a large size zigzag stitch. This gives a decorative effect and also stops the seams from gaping during wear. If you do not have a swing-needle machine, straight-stitch close to the edge of each shape. When all seams have been stitched, trim the edges of the leather and calico level all around, trimming the end of the calico to the same shape as the largest brown leather shape. Working on the wrong side, lightly coat the calico with latex adhesive, then fold the sides of the belt to the centre on the wrong side, butting the edges together down the centre and folding the large end shape as shown on the dotted lines in the diagram. Hammer the belt lightly all over to make the folds lie flat and leave to dry thoroughly. Starting at the shaped end and using the eyelet punch, place an eyelet in the centre of each strip for about eight strips, then measure the belt around the waist allowing a 2in turning on the buckle end plus the amount you want to overlap through the buckle. Trim off the surplus at the buckle end, then place an eyelet in the centre, 2in from the cut edge. Trim the cut end to a point, slip the buckle on to the belt, pushing the prong through the eyelet and folding the pointed end down on to the back of the belt. Using contact adhesive, carefully stick end in place to the belt and allow it to dry thoroughly. To make a slide for holding the free end of the belt in position during wear, cut a strip of leather about $4\frac{1}{2}$in by 1in and stick the sides to the centre on the wrong side with latex adhesive. Wrap this around the belt to estimate the correct length, then skive and stick the ends together with contact adhesive. Slip this small

loop on to the belt and slide it down towards the buckle end.

A leather jacket is one of the more difficult garments to make, so do not attempt it unless you are really sure of your dressmaking skill and are used to making quite complicated things in leather.

This type of jacket will last a good many years, but a lot of work goes into making it, so make it worthwhile by using good quality leather. Do not choose too trendy a design, or you will find that it tends to look dated long before the leather begins to show any signs of wear. Wear signs will occur first in the lining fabric and in the seams, so buy really good quality lining and a strong Polyester or silk thread for stitching all the seams. The man's jacket pictured on p140 was adapted from a purchased pattern (Butterick 6464). This particular one was chosen because the body of the jacket is divided into several vertical panels and a yoke. These shapes can be fitted economically on to the leather skins for cutting out. The amount of leather needed for this jacket was five large sheep skins (approximately 7sq ft each) but you could omit the belt and pockets and save about half a skin. Even though good quality leather is not cheap, this jacket was made for just under half the price of a similar purchased one.

The pattern was originally designed with frog fastenings, but I substituted a zip-fastener. I also rounded off the pointed corners of the collar to make them easier to turn right side out after stitching. The pockets were moved forwards about $3\frac{1}{2}$in from their original position so that they crossed only one of the vertical jacket seams. This made stitching them on much easier. The pattern gave instructions for a lined yoke only, but if a leather jacket is left unlined little bits of leather rub off from the flesh side and tend to spoil the garments worn underneath, so in order to prevent this I cut out a lining following the main jacket pattern, and made it up in the same way, omitting the pockets, collar and belt and allowing extra for a box pleat down the centre back for ease during wear.

It is an extremely good idea to make up a pattern as complicated as this in handicraft felt, tacking all the main seams together and trying the garment on. You can then adjust the pattern for a perfect fit before starting to cut

Man's leather jacket

141

out your leather and thereby prevent any costly mistakes. Unpick the seams in the felt and use the sections to cut out your leather, marking the right side of each shape with chalk to make sure you cut out a left and a right side of all pattern pieces.

Arrange the shapes on the right side of the leather and mark around them with chalk. Take care to avoid any large flaws or marks in the leather and get similar thicknesses for identical pattern shapes. The collar and collar band are best cut from a thinner part of the skins to make them easier to turn right side out after stitching and less bulky for top-stitching. Cut out all the shapes, then transfer all the pattern markings to the wrong side of the leather with chalk, using the original paper patterns as guides for notches and other markings. Make up the jacket following the printed instructions but with amendments where necessary. For example, tacking is not possible but you can stab-stitch within the seam allowances with a gloving needle to hold the shapes together ready for the final stitching and, of course, clothes-pegs and bulldog clips can also be used. To prevent the top layer of leather stretching under the machine foot when seaming, it is wise to place a piece of cotton tape along the seam line on top of the leather and stitch through this as well as the leather as described on p108. The tape can be carefully cut away afterwards if necessary, but it does help to avoid the

Yoke front and pocket of man's jacket

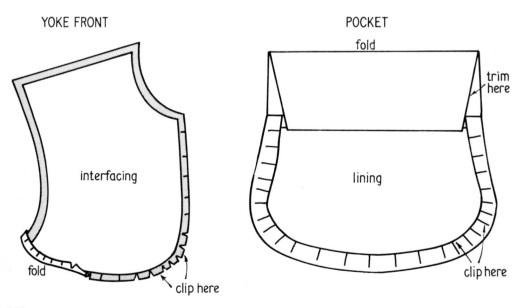

YOKE FRONT

interfacing

fold

clip here

POCKET

fold

trim here

lining

clip here

tendency for seams to curl and pucker down one side.

When a seam has been stitched, hammer and stick it flat before going on to the next one. Trim off excess bulk from the seams if they are to be top-stitched or the sewing machine may not be able to cope with the extra thickness, especially where seams cross one another.

For the jacket pictured on p140 it was necessary to attach the yoke in a slightly different way to that described in the printed instructions supplied with the pattern. In order to make it easier I cut out the yoke shapes, minus the seam allowances, from hair canvas and stuck these on to the wrong side of the leather yoke shapes with latex adhesive around the edges of the canvas. I then clipped into the seam allowances along the lower edges of the yoke shapes, turned up the seam allowances like hems and glued them in place to the hair canvas with latex adhesive, as shown in the diagram. When the lower panels of the bodice were assembled and top-stitched, the yoke was carefully stuck in place with contact adhesive, overlapping the seam allowances, and then top-stitched to hold it firmly in position. This method prevents any unsightly puckering of the yoke or bodice which sometimes happens if the seams are stitched in the normal way when they may stretch during assembly.

Pockets

Cut out two main pocket shapes from the lining, then trim the seam allowances from these and stick one in place to the wrong side of each pocket with latex adhesive used sparingly around the edges. Join the pocket band to each pocket as described in the pattern instructions, then clip into the seam allowance around the sides and base of the pocket. Fold this seam allowance over and stick smoothly to the lining with latex adhesive. Mitre the corners of the top hem allowance, as shown in the diagram, then fold this over and stick in place with latex adhesive. Top-stitch along either side of the pocket band seam to hold the top hem firmly in place. To attach the pockets to the jacket; spread a little contact adhesive around the seam allowance at the sides and base of the pocket, then while it is still wet, place the pocket carefully in position on the jacket front. Press down well and leave for a while to let the adhesive dry thoroughly, then top-stitch around the sides and base of the pocket about $\frac{1}{8}$in from the edge. Make another line

143

of stitching $\frac{1}{8}$in inside this first line for added strength and decoration. Attach the other pocket in the same way.

Shoulder, side, centre back and sleeve seams are stitched in the usual way, opened out, hammered flat and stuck in place with latex adhesive. To inset the sleeve into the armhole, clip into the seam allowance around the top of the armhole to help ease in the sleeve. Match all markings and stab-stitch the sleeve in position, easing as you go and holding temporarily in place with clothes-pegs or bulldog clips. Machine-stitch the sleeve in position along the seam line, then stitch again, within the seam allowance about $\frac{1}{4}$in inside the first line of stitching. Trim the seam where necessary, then hammer and stick the seam towards the bodice of the jacket with latex adhesive, clipping into the seam allowance where necessary to obtain a smooth fit.

Make up the lining in the same way as the jacket, making a box pleat down the centre back of the yoke and bodice with the extra fabric allowed for during the cutting out. Press all the bodice seams open. Yoke seams should be pressed upwards and shoulder seams towards the sleeve at the armhole. Then trim off the hem allowance from the lower edges of the bodice and sleeves. Arrange the lining inside the jacket and, making sure that it does not pull or drag anywhere, with latex adhesive stick around the edges of the lining and press on to the jacket.

Instead of stitching the front facing in place down the entire front of the jacket, just stitch about 1in at either end, then turn back the seam allowances and stick them down to make hems on both the jacket fronts and the facing fronts. Turn the facing to the inside of the jacket, carefully turning out the corners with a pencil. Insert the zip-fastener into the front of the jacket between the facing and the jacket front and stick it in place with contact adhesive, leaving the teeth exposed so that the folded front edge of the jacket is clear of the zip slide and will not get rubbed and worn each time the zip is opened or closed. Carefully stick down the jacket hem, facing and sleeve hem with latex adhesive, then top-stitch down the front of the jacket and around the hem to hold firmly in place and to act as a decoration. Also top-stitch around the hem of each sleeve. Make up the collar and collar band according to the instructions supplied with the pattern, taking great care in turning the collar right side out. Do not trim off too much from the outer seam allowance or you may have trouble

Patchwork cape

144

in top-stitching with your machine. Treating the top edge of the jacket and the lining as one fabric, attach the collar band as described in the pattern instructions.

PATCHWORK LEATHERWORK CAPE

Never throw away your offcuts unless they are really tiny, and here is the reason why! This cape is made from the offcuts of several years' work; they were carefully sorted out and then the thinnest and most supple pieces were used to make the main part of the cape. A project like this should not be lightly undertaken—the cutting out of the shapes alone took several days. The best way to start on a job of this magnitude is to cut out the patches from your offcuts as you discard them from other projects and keep them in small bags of 100 so that you can easily estimate when you have enough to start making something. This cape took about 1,500 diamond-shaped patches, each one roughly $2\frac{1}{4}$in long and $1\frac{1}{4}$in wide. Half of these were in the same dark brown colour as the collar and yoke (the remnants of the man's jacket) and these have been arranged so as to occur alternately with the other colours to give a feeling of unity throughout the design.

Materials
Different-coloured leather offcuts cut into patches
A large piece of leather for the collar and yoke
Thin, pre-shrunk fabric for the backing (an old sheet is ideal)
Latex adhesive
Silk thread in the main colour (you will need about twelve reels)
$2\frac{1}{2}$yd of 36in-wide lining fabric
Contact adhesive
A piece of hair canvas for the collar interfacing
A 20in-long heavy duty cardigan zip

Method
When you estimate that you have enough leather patches saved up, make a pattern from the diagram (scale: one square represents 2in) and use this to cut out two shapes A, two shapes B and one shape C from the backing fabric. Reverse one shape A left to right and mark the right side of both these pieces to prevent any mistakes.

Starting at the front straight edge of shapes A, and in

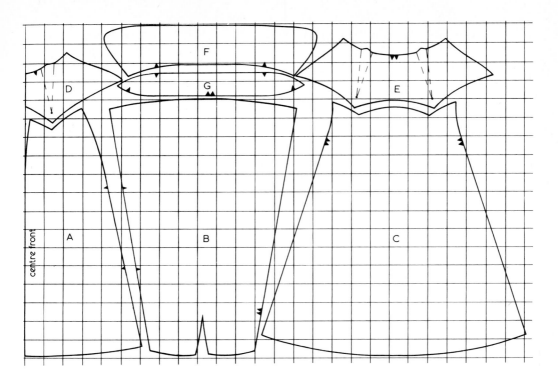

Pattern for a patchwork cape. One square represents 4sq in

the centre of pieces B and C, stick a line of diamond patches from top to bottom in a straight line, then add the other shapes to the sides of this and continue them outwards in vertical lines until the whole of the backing fabric of each piece is covered. Use the latex adhesive sparingly to stick them down, paying particular attention to the points of the diamond shapes. Use any incomplete or damaged shapes for the very edge of each section. When all the diamonds are firmly stuck in place, thread the machine and set it to a fairly large zigzag stitch, then stitch along each row of joins to anchor the edges of the patches firmly to the backing. When the patchwork sections are all made up in this way, it is a good idea to soften them by folding and rolling them all over in several directions; this will give a softly creased all-over effect and will prevent the cape from being too stiff the first few times it is worn. You can also give the leather surface a coat of colourless wax polish to help merge the different textures of the various patches and to help make it more weatherproof.

To Make up the Cape

From the large pieces of plain leather cut out two front yoke sections D, one back yoke section E, two collars F and two collar bands G. Use the thinner parts of the leather for the two collar bands and the lower edges of the collars since all these thicknesses will have to be stitched together in one seam. Also cut out a collar shape from hair canvas, trim away the seam allowance all round and stick it carefully with latex adhesive to the wrong side of one of the collar shapes. With right sides facing, join one piece A to one piece B down the notched side, leaving the area between the notches open to make the front hand vent of the cape. Stitch these pieces together with a $\frac{1}{2}$in seam, then open the seam out and stick it down flat with latex adhesive. Repeat with the other pieces A and B. Spread a little latex adhesive on the wrong side of the lower edges of both pieces D, clip into the seam allowances and turn up a $\frac{1}{2}$in hem along the two lower edges of each piece, easing around the curves. Stitch the darts in both these pieces, turn the darts towards the shoulder seams and stick them down as flat as possible. Spread a little contact adhesive on the turned hem of each of these pieces and stick them carefully in place to the top of the front and side joined sections A and B, matching the centre fronts and curved edges. When the adhesive has dried, top-stitch the yoke in place with two rows of stitching spaced about $\frac{1}{8}$in apart.

With right sides facing, join the sides of the back section of the cape C to the two side sections B with $\frac{1}{2}$in seams. Clip into the curves where necessary, open the seams and stick them down flat with latex adhesive. Turn up the lower hem of the back yoke section E, stitch the darts and then attach the yoke to the back and sides of the cape in the same way that the front yoke was attached, matching centres and curved edges. With right sides facing, stitch together the back and front shoulder seams of the cape, extending the dart at the outer edge of the shoulder and gradually tapering it to nothing down the centre of piece B. If you end this dart too abruptly you will get an awkward-looking point on the shoulder of the cape. Trim neck edges, centre front and lower edge of the cape level all round.

Make up the lining in exactly the same way as the cape, leaving the area between the notches on pieces A and B open for the front hand vents. Before you insert the lining into the cape, strengthen the top and bottom of each hand vent on the wrong side of the leather by sticking a short length of tape across it at right angles to the seam. This will prevent the seam from splitting during wear. Trim off 1in from the lower edge of the lining and ½in from each centre front edge. With right sides facing, join the lining to the cape at the centre front edges with a ½in seam, then turn the lining and cape to the right side. Fold the centre front edges of the leather so that the stitching line is about ¼in from the folded edge and stick this fold carefully in place with latex adhesive so that the lining will not bag at the centre front. Carefully stick the lower edge of the lining to the cape, 1in from the edge of the leather and backing fabric, then turn up a 1in hem all around the lower edge, mitring the two front corners, and stick firmly in place, hammering the fold well to make it lie flat. Carefully stick the top edge of the lining to the top edge of the cape with latex adhesive, taking care not to stretch the lining or it will pull the top edges of the leather out of shape. Use contact adhesive very sparingly to stick the folded edges of the lining to the edges of the hand vents, about ¼in from the folded edges of the leather; then, working on the right side of the cape, top-stitch around the hand vents to anchor the lining firmly in place.

Stitch the two collar   sections together around the sides and top, clip into the seam allowance where necessary, turn right side out and hammer flat. Then top-stitch all around the turned edges. With right sides facing and notches matched, join one edge of each collar band to each side of the neck edge of the collar with a ½in seam, trim the seam, and turn the collar band down away from the collar. With right sides facing, stitch the opposite edge of one of these bands to the neck edge of the cape, matching the notches and stitching through both the leather and the lining. (You will probably have to stitch the very end of each of the seams by hand, using a glover's needle, since the several thicknesses of leather may not pass under the machine foot.) Trim away the seam allowance from the pointed ends of the collar band, collar and top of cape at each front edge, then clip into the remaining seam allowance at intervals to enable it to lie flat. With latex adhesive stick these seam allowances

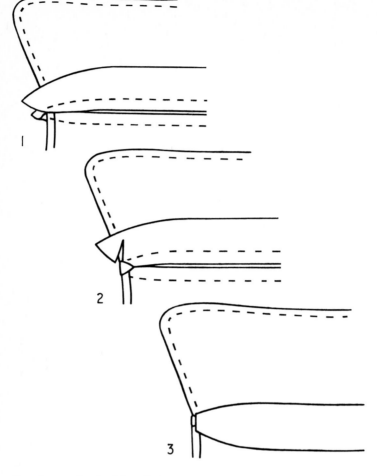

firmly to the inside of the collar band (1), then turn the
pointed end of the stitched collar band to the inside and
stick in place with contact adhesive (2). Finally trim off
the point from the inside collar band and turn it down
over all the seam edges (3), sticking it in place mainly
with latex adhesive, but using contact adhesive for extra
strength at each end.

Using contact adhesive sparingly, stick the zip in place
down the front of the cape, starting just below the yoke
seam, then top-stitch down the front of the cape and
around the hem to hold the zip and hem in place and
emphasise the edges of the garment. You can, if you wish,
add a button and loop to the front of the yoke section,
or a frog fastening, or you can leave it to be worn slightly
open.

An attractive and inexpensive toy can be made from smaller offcuts, stitched in place either by hand or machine. This ball is ideal for a baby or young child since it is soft and resilient and will not bounce and cause damage. Twelve pentagon shapes are needed to make a ball, and you can choose the size to fit your offcuts.

Materials
Offcuts of suede or leather in five colours
Pre-shrunk cotton tape
Latex adhesive
Silk thread in predominant colour
Kapok for stuffing

Method
Make a pentagon template from a circle (1). (The template used for the ball pictured on p153 was made from

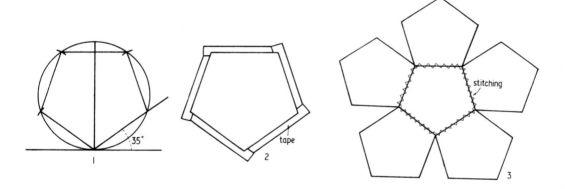

Making a football from pentagon shapes

a 3¼in-diameter circle and the finished ball was about 16in in circumference). Use the template to cut out twelve suede or leather patches, then arrange these into two groups of six, each group in the shape of a flower with five petals and a centre. Take care in this arrangement not to get identical colours touching. Take one of the centre shapes and stick short lengths of tape to each side on the wrong side (2), then stick the 'petals' around this (3) and zigzag or hand-stitch them in place. (The tape is for extra strength and also to prevent the edges stretching as you stitch.) Now join each 'petal' to its neighbour using tape and stitching as before. When all

151

these seams are stitched you should have a bowl shape.
Make up the other group of shapes in the same way, then
fit both shapes together and stick with tape and then
stitch as before, leaving two short seams open for stuffing.
If you are stitching by machine the last few seams become
increasingly difficult to sew and you must take great care
not to catch some other part of the ball in the seams.
Stuff very firmly with kapok, pushing the ball into a
smooth round shape as you go. To close remaining seams,
lay a small piece of fabric smoothly over the kapok in the
opening then carefully stick the open seam in position to
this. When the adhesive has dried, stitch the seams firmly
by hand. To imitate the machine zigzag, first oversew
along both seams with a glover's needle taking fairly
large stitches, then unthread this needle and replace
with a blunt harness needle. Retrace your steps, using
the harness needle in the holes made by the glover's
needle, in a zigzag pattern. Finish off securely.

SUEDE MOUSE

This amusing little chap is made from offcuts in two
different colours. His body consists of three identical
shapes joined together by machine or hand-stitching and
he is filled with kapok to make a smooth, firm shape.

Materials
Offcuts of suede in two different colours
Matching silk thread in both colours
Latex adhesive
Kapok for stuffing

Method
Make paper patterns of the ear and body shapes from
diagram 1 (scale: one square represents 1sq in) and use
the large pattern to cut out three shapes from the main
colour suede. Using latex adhesive sparingly, stick some
main colour and contrast scraps together, back-to-back,
then cut out two small ear shapes from this double-sided
suede. Cut also a strip 12in long for the tail from the main
colour and two small circles for eyes and a small triangle
for the nose from a contrast colour. Select the two best-
looking large shapes for the sides of the body and arrange
them nose-to-nose on the table, then cut a small slot in
each for the ears, following the marking on the diagram.

Suede mouse and suede football

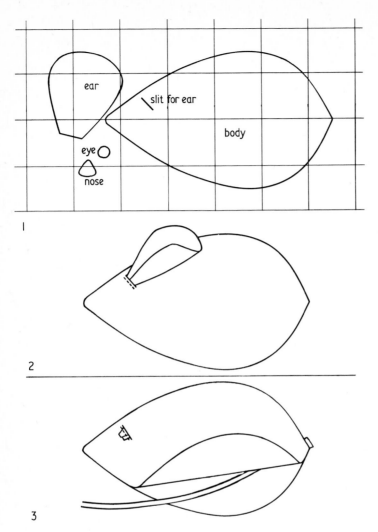

1

2

3

Fold each ear in half with the contrast side inside and insert one into each slot (2). Stick firmly in place on the wrong side with latex adhesive, then top-stitch as shown. With right sides facing, stitch these two main shapes together along the top side, taking care not to catch the ears in the seam. Start at the nose and work along the seam, sandwiching the tail in between at the other end (3). With right sides facing, stitch one side of the third shape in place, then stitch about 1in of the other side in position at the nose and tail ends. Carefully turn the mouse to the right side through the opening in the side, and using contrast thread, stitch the whiskers in

Spotted suede horse

154

place at each side of the pointed nose. Dab a little latex adhesive inside the nose area to anchor the whiskers firmly in place. Stuff the mouse firmly with kapok and stitch the remaining seam to close. Stick the eyes and nose carefully in position with latex adhesive.

SPOTTED SUEDE HORSE

This horse toy stands about 10in high to the tip of its ears,

and would make an ideal mascot for a horse-mad child. The mane and tail are made from fringed contrast suede, but the spots have been painted on with special suede dye to add finishing touches.

Materials
Largish pieces of soft suede in the main colour
Matching sewing thread
Scraps of contrast colour suede
Clear contact adhesive
Kapok for stuffing
Small scrap of stiff card
Dylon suede dye in two toning colours

Pattern for a spotted suede horse. One square represents 1sq in

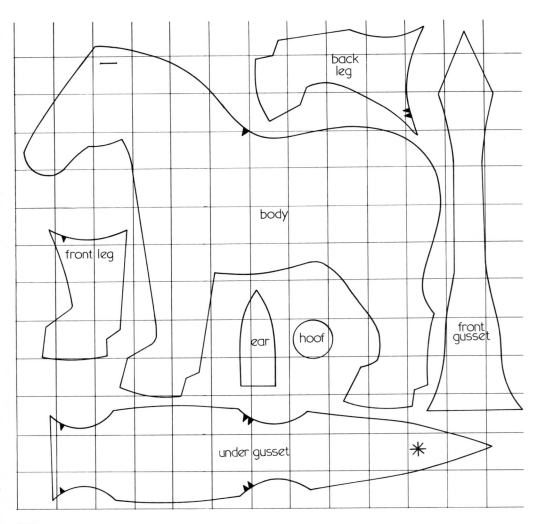

Method

Use the diagram (scale: one square represents 1sq in) to make paper patterns for all the parts, then use these to cut out two body shapes (reversing one left to right for the opposite side), two back and two front legs, reversing one of each, one under-gusset and one front gusset from the main colour suede. From the scraps left over, stick some largish pieces back-to-back to make a thicker, double-sided suede and cut out two ears from this. From the contrast suede cut out a strip 7in by 5in for the tail and two strips 5in by 3in for the mane Also cut out four hoof shapes from stiff card and also from single, main colour suede.

Trim the 7in by 5in piece of contrast suede into a fringe down its length to within $\frac{1}{2}$in of one short end, then wind this end up like a swiss roll to make the tail. Tie a length of thread tightly around it where the fringe begins, then carefully clip into the outer layer of the 'swiss-roll' part so that it can be spread out and anchored in place inside the horse. Using a sharp craft knife, cut a star-shaped opening in the under-gusset as shown on the diagram, then insert the solid part of the tail into this, fan out the clipped edges and stick them firmly in place to the inside with clear adhesive. You can reinforce the tail by stitching if you wish. Cut a slit in the top of each head shape as shown in the diagram. Fold each ear shape in half at the base and insert into the slit with the fold facing towards the back of the head. Stick firmly in place with clear adhesive and reinforce with stitching if necessary. With right sides facing join the legs to the under-gusset, matching notches and taking seams about $\frac{1}{4}$in wide, then join the short straight ends of the under-gusset and the front gusset in the same way. With right sides facing, join one side of the under-gusset and legs to one body shape, stitching first the belly and inside leg seams, then the back of the back legs up to the end of the gusset, then the front of the front legs, the neck, around the head to the top of the forehead, easing where necessary and clipping into curves to make stitching easier. Leave the lower ends of the hooves open for stuffing. Stitch the other body shape to the other side of the gusset in the same way, then while the horse is still inside out stitch the back seam from the end of the gusset to the notch at the base of the neck. Turn down a $\frac{1}{4}$in hem at each side of the neck seam and stick firmly in place with clear adhesive. Clip into all angles and corners around the seams and carefully turn the horse right side out.

Firmly pack the kapok into the head, neck and body through the neck opening, taking care to get a smooth firm filling. Trim the two 5in by 3in contrast pieces of suede into fringes to within $\frac{1}{2}$in of one long side of each, then stick them firmly to the inside of each hemmed neck edge. When you are satisfied that the horse is firmly filled with stuffing, spread a little adhesive along the inner edge of each mane section and press them firmly together to close the neck edge. Using a pencil, stuff the legs very firmly, one at a time, bearing in mind that they will have to take the full weight of the body without sagging, then insert a circle of card into the open end, clip into the lower edge of the hoof all around for $\frac{1}{4}$in, turn this over the card and stick firmly in place. Cover the clipped edges by sticking a circle of suede to the base of the hoof and trimming it to fit exactly. Carefully paint on the eyes, nostrils, hooves and spots with the suede dye, using a fine watercolour brush. Leave to dry thoroughly, then brush up the texture of the suede all over with a suede brush or clothes-brush.

SPECTACLE CASE WITH FRAME

This simple but attractive spectacle case is made from two offcuts of bright scarlet suede attached to a purchased metal frame. The applied decoration consists of a selection of eyelets and studs in gilt and nickel finish which have been inserted into the leather in a pattern of simple flowerhead shapes.

Materials
Two pieces of suede or leather at least 6$\frac{1}{2}$in by 3$\frac{1}{2}$in
Matching silk thread
Purchased frame 2$\frac{1}{2}$in wide and 1$\frac{1}{2}$in deep (closed)
Latex adhesive
Clear adhesive
Selection of studs and eyelets
Scrap of fabric or leather to line studded area

Method
Make a pattern from the diagram (scale: one square represents 1sq in) and use this to cut out two pieces of

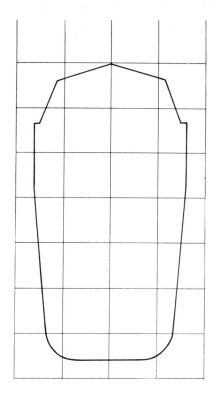

*Pattern for a spectacle case.
One square represents 1 sq in*

suede. Arrange the studs and eyelets on the right side of one of these and fix them in position with the tool provided. Stick the piece of lining fabric or leather in place over the wrong side of the decorated area with latex adhesive. Alternatively, cut out shapes of your choice from contrast-coloured leather and suede, arrange these on the right side of the case and stitch or stick in place. With right sides facing, join the two pieces of suede together down the sides and around the base with a narrow seam, then turn the case to the right side and pull firmly into shape around the edges. Insert the case into the opened frame, spread a little clear adhesive around the inside of the frame and press the suede firmly into place. Leave to dry thoroughly. When the adhesive is dry, thread a fine glover's needle or other sharp fine needle with double thread and stitch the case firmly to the frame through the small holes provided in the edge of the frame.

LEATHER AND SUEDE FLOWERS

Make a pretty bouquet of different-coloured flowers from some of your smallish offcuts. They look most attractive

159

160

when arranged in a vase with some sprigs of greenery, or with dried copper beech leaves and grasses.

Materials (for one flower)
A scrap of leather or suede about 3in square
.A large glass or wooden bead in a toning colour
Clear adhesive
A 12in length of stiff florist's wire

Method
Draw the flower shape in the diagram (scale: one square

Pattern for leather and suede flowers. One square represents 1sq in

represents 1sq in) on a piece of stiff card and cut it out; then use this as a template to cut out the flowerhead shape from leather or suede. On the right side of this apply a little clear adhesive to the centre base of each petal, as shown on the diagram, then pinch the petal in half down its length with the thumb and forefinger to enclose the adhesive and make a small pleat. Hold this in position until the adhesive has set, then repeat with the other four petals. You should now have a flower which looks as though it is just about to open out from a bud. Turn back the ends of the petals so that the flower looks a little more open (look at the photograph on p160), but take care to treat it gently and not strain the adhesive at the folded pleats. Thread the bead on one end of the wire and twist the wire to hold the bead firmly in place.

Leather and suede flowers   Then apply a little adhesive to the base of the bead where

161

it joins the wire stem. Make a small hole in the centre of the flower and thread the stem into it until the bead sits well down in the centre of the flower where the adhesive will hold it permanently in place. Make the other flowers in the same way.

CLAMSHELL PATCHWORK CUSHION

This suede cushion cover is made from pieces that are

4in or more in diameter. Subtle browns and fawns are mixed together here to give a sophisticated, rather Art Deco effect.

Materials
Offcuts of suede in different colours
Latex adhesive
16in square of calico or other thin, cheap cotton fabric
16in square of plain fabric for the back of the cushion
Matching silk thread
15in zip-fastener
15in-square cushion pad

Method
Use the diagram to make a template from a 4in-diameter circle, then cut out thirty-six patches from the suede. Select five of these in different colours and divide them in

Making a clamshell template from a circle

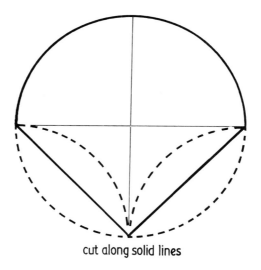

cut along solid lines

half down the centre to make half-patches for the ends of the alternate rows. Iron the calico well all over and rule into 2in squares, marking the lines with a pencil to act as guidelines. Lay out all the patches on a flat surface and arrange the colours in a pleasing pattern before transferring them to the calico. To do this, spread a little latex adhesive on to the top row of squares, then arrange the first row of patches in place with points A positioned in a straight line along the top edge of the calico, and *Patchwork suede cushion* points B positioned where alternate vertical lines meet

163

the first horizontal line. Press down firmly, then start the second row of patches, overlapping the first row where indicated by the curved dotted line on the diagram. Continue sticking patches in this way until they are all used up then, when the adhesive is thoroughly dry, press the square well all over on the wrong side with a medium-hot iron.

Thread your sewing machine with the silk thread and top-stitch around the top curved edge of each patch close to the edge. I used a medium-sized zigzag stitch, but a straight stitch would do just as well. When all the shapes are firmly stitched down, press well again on the wrong side and leave lying flat to cool. Meanwhile, turn under a $\frac{1}{2}$in hem down one side of the backing fabric and stitch one side of the zip-fastener to this, arranging the fabric so that the folded edge lies straight along the centre of the zip teeth. Trim the suede edges level with the edges of the calico square, then with right sides facing, stitch the suede and fabric squares together along the zip side with a $\frac{1}{4}$in seam, treating the zip tape as the edge of the fabric. Open the zip a little way for easy turning later on, then stitch the other three sides of the square with a $\frac{1}{2}$in seam. Trim the seam and clip away excess fabric and suede from the corners, then turn to the right side through the zip opening. Push the corners of the cover firmly into shape from the inside, using the blunt end of a pencil; then insert the cushion pad and close the zip.

Cleaning and Care

The shiny surfaces of most grain leathers help to protect them against most kinds of soiling and this can be further assisted by treating them with care and following some basic commonsense rules regarding general care and cleaning.

Remove any marks or spills as soon as they occur with a damp cloth or sponge, never use an abrasive, and wipe away any traces of water you have used immediately. If a garment is worn in the rain, dry as much water from the surface as you can with a soft, clean cloth or a piece of kitchen paper and then allow the garment to dry slowly away from direct heat. Never try to hurry the drying process or the leather could become hard and brittle. Treat leather suitcases, bags, etc in the same way; do not allow marks or spills to remain on the surface for long or they may make a permanent stain. When not in use store all leather items in a well-ventilated, dry place avoiding extremes of temperature. Do not store leather in polythene bags; if you want to protect it from dust make a bag from calico or other cheap cotton fabric, or use a large paper bag. This discourages mildew and allows the leather to breathe inside.

There are several products on the market which you can

165

use to keep grain leather clean and in good condition. Probably the most well-known of these is Propert's Saddle Soap, made by Propert Ltd, Burlington Lane, London W4 2RN, and stocked by most shoe repairers and saddlers. This is a special soap in a tin which is applied with a damp sponge, worked into a rich lather and rubbed well into the surface of the leather. The surplus lather is removed with a nearly dry sponge and the leather is then polished with a soft cloth. Other products include Leather Groom by Orkin Ltd, 50 Central Buildings, 24 Southwark Street, London SE1 1UG, which is an aerosol foam, and also CEE BEE Hide Food, made by Connolly Bros (Curriers) Ltd, 39-43 Chalton Street, Euston Road, London NW1 1JE. When using any polish or cleaner on leather, test a small area first in an inconspicuous place to make sure there is no adverse reaction. This is particularly important on items you have stained and polished yourself.

SUEDE

Generally speaking, suede becomes soiled fairly quickly because of the texture of the surface. The marks which show up first are usually grease marks which attract dust from the atmosphere and become discoloured. Care should be taken to protect suede from any kind of oil or grease and it is wise always to wear a scarf in the neck of a suede coat as a precaution, and to avoid preparing food or cooking whilst wearing a suede garment. Constant handling of suede articles should also be avoided if possible.

Many dry marks can be removed from the surface of suede by carefully rubbing with a pencil eraser, but try this out first on an inconspicuous part of the garment and do not rub too hard or you may damage the surface. If you get caught in the rain, blot off as much water as you can then hang the garment to dry slowly, away from direct heat. When it is almost dry, brush it gently with a suede brush to restore the nap. Crumpled garments can be hung in a steamy bathroom for a while and then brushed to freshen them up. Spills should be blotted off immediately with tissue or kitchen roll and it is a wise precaution to treat suede garments with a colourless spray-on barrier such as Swade Guard by Orkin Ltd, 50 Central Buildings, 24 Southwark Street, London SE1 1UG, which forms a seal against soiling. Some grease marks can be removed with a proprietary grease solvent, but always try it out first in an unseen area to test for any colour reactions.

When the time comes for all-over cleaning, or if a garment is accidentally very badly marked, consult a specialist leather and suede cleaning firm. The Association of British Launderers and Cleaners, 22 Lancaster Gate, London W2 3LL, will supply the address of your nearest one if you write to their Services Adviser.

WASHABLE SUEDE

Most washable suede should have a leaflet supplied with it telling you how it should be washed and whether or not it can be cleaned by ordinary dry-cleaning processes. The basic rules for washing this type of suede are as follows. Use only soap-free detergents and make sure they are thoroughly dissolved before immersing the garment. Wash at a temperature of 40°C (104°F)—this will be water which is pleasantly warm to the hand but not hot. Do not leave the garment to soak but keep it moving all the time or it may develop patchy stains. Rinse very well as this is most important. Do not wring. The suede can be spun-dried for a short spin and should then be hung to dry away from direct heat. Gently ease the garment into shape whilst it is drying, then when it is thoroughly dry, iron it carefully using a protective dry cloth and setting the iron to a wool temperature. Finally gently brush up the nap with a suede brush.

Stockists and Useful Addresses

LEATHER MANUFACTURERS AND SUPPLIERS

Here is a list of some leather manufacturers and suppliers who operate a postal service. They will send cuttings of the various types and colours of leather that they stock on request, together with lists of prices and approximate sizes of hides and skins.

Alma Leather Ltd, Bolton House, 18–30 Clerkenwell Road, London EC1 5PR. Personal callers only.

Anthony Booth, Ltd, Galley Field Industrial Estate, Radley Road, Abingdon, Berkshire.

Connolly Bros (Curriers) Ltd, 39–43 Chalton Street, Euston Road, London NW1 1JE. Personal callers welcome. This firm carries a very wide range of all types of leather, so if you write to them state the type you are seeking so that they can send selected cuttings only.

Dryad Handicrafts Ltd, Northgates, Leicester, LE1 4QR. Ask for their catalogue; they supply tools and adhesives as well as many other craft materials.

The Light Leather Company Ltd, 18 Newman Street, London W1P 3HD. Personal callers only.

A. L. Maugham & Co Ltd, 5 Fazakerley Street, Liverpool L3 9DN.

Quality First, 27 Court Drive, Stanmore, Middlesex.

Redpath, Campbell and Partners Ltd, Cheapside, Stroud, Gloucestershire GL5 3DG. They also supply bags of offcuts for patchwork.

The Tannery Shop, Gomshall, Surrey. Personal callers welcome. Suppliers of washable 'Suede 66'.

Leather and suede for clothing can also be purchased from the dress fabric departments of some of the larger stores, such as Liberty of Regent Street, London W1R 6AH and Bentalls of Kingston, Surrey.

168

Tools

Specialist leatherwork tools are manufactured by Taylor & Co (Tools) Ltd, 54 Old Street, London EC1V 9AL. Ask for their catalogue and price list; they will send items by post.

Dryad Handicrafts and A. L. Maugham (both listed in the leather section) supply some tools also.

Leather, tools, stains and fittings from Batchelor & Co, Netherhall Gardens, London NW3 5RL. Write for a catalogue and price list.

Adhesives

Copydex Ltd, 1 Torquay Street, London W2 5EL, make latex adhesive in tubes, 4oz jars (with brush) and 10oz or 1pt tins. This should not, however, be used on garments you intend to have dry-cleaned.

Bostick 1 clear adhesive can be used here. It is manufactured by Bostik Ltd, Ulverscroft Road, Leicester LE4 6VW.

White paste is made under the trade name 'Gloy' by Associated Adhesives Ltd, London E12 5JW. This type of paste is also made by Dryad Handicrafts under their own brandname.

All these adhesives can be obtained from most Do-It-Yourself shops, hardware stores and handicraft shops.

Other Items

Patchwork templates are made by JEM Patchwork Templates, Pyrton, Watlington, Oxon OX9 5AP and distributed through handicraft shops and large stores.

The 'F. A. Staite' glove pattern, moccasin and slipper patterns can be obtained from Mrs Staite (Patterns), Carlidnack, Mawnan Smith, near Falmouth, or from handicraft shops.

Buckles, clasps and other findings can be found in the catalogue of Taylor & Co (Tools) Ltd, listed above.

Fashion buttons, buckles and evening-bag frames can be bought from the haberdashery departments of most large stores. (The frames for the spectacle case and the evening bag shown in this book were obtained from John Lewis, Oxford Street, London W1A 1EX.)

Eyelets, press-studs and similar fastenings are made by Newey Bros Ltd, PO Box 277, Robin Hood Lane, Hall Green, Birmingham B28 0JG, and supplied in kits with the tools to fix them in large stores and handicraft shops.

Silk thread made in West Germany by Gütermann and stocked by most large stores including John Lewis.

THONGING AND LACING

Dryad Handicrafts (as already mentioned).
Homecraft, 27 Trinity Road, London SW17 7SF.
D. Murray & Co, 64 High Street, Winslow, Bucks MK18 3DQ.

BUCKLES AND OTHER FINDINGS

James Alden Ltd, 398 City Road, London EC1V 2QA.
Rose Fittings Ltd, 337 City Road, London EC1V 2559.

STAINS AND DYES

Dylon International Ltd, London SE26 5HD (makers of Miss Dylon Suede Dye obtainable from most large stores).
Gedge & Co (Clerkenwell) Ltd, 88 St John Street, London EC1M 4EJ. Personal callers only.

List of Leather Terms

Aniline   Vegetable tanned hide or split hide used for bags, cases, folios, etc. Has the original grain showing, not covered by any pigmented finish

Antelope   Fine, soft leather made from gazelle or antelope skins with a suede finish

Back   The main, centre part of a hide when the two bellies have been trimmed away from the sides

Basil   Vegetable tanned sheepskin, sometimes undyed, but always left with a natural grain for modelling and tooling

Beaver Lamb   The skin of a sheep or lamb which has been dressed with the wool still on (see shearling)

Belly   The two sides of a hide or skin which are usually the weakest and thinnest part

Boarded   Leather which has been folded and creased, by hand or by machine, to give an all-over softly creased effect

Buckskin   Soft suede leather made from the skin of a deer

Buffing   Sanding off the grain surface of the leather with fine abrasive to remove any scars and imperfections in the surface

Butt   The best part of a hide after the bellies and shoulders have been removed

Calf   Leather from young bovine animals, very supple and hard wearing. Used for high quality bags, luggage and some clothing

Cape   Grain gloving or clothing leather from South Africa, produced from the skins of hair sheep as opposed to wool sheep

Chamois   Traditionally leather made from the skin of the Chamois goat, but these days usually sheepskin processed in a way that introduces a lot of oil to keep it supple

Channeling   Cutting a groove with a race to make a seam lie flat (see p25), usually reducing the thickness of the leather by half

Chrome Tanned   Leather tanned by using chromium salts

Coach Hide   High quality leather used mainly for luggage. The very best is usually aniline dyed and retains all its natural grain

Creasing   Marking a line with a creaser (see p41–2), usually round the edges of cut edge work

Crocodile   The skin from reptiles of the crocodile and alligator family. The belly is the part generally used, the back being too hard and horny to be workable

Crust Leather   Leather which has been tanned and dried but not dyed or finished; usually applied to skins rather than hides

Cut Edge Work   Items made in such a way that the cut edges of the leather are left unturned, then stained and burnished or polished

Doeskin   Very fine, soft glove leather, usually white or cream in colour, made from lamb or sheepskin split

Edge Finishing   Staining, varnishing, burnishing or waxing cut edges.

E.I.   An abbreviation of East India, applying to all types of leather produced in India and surrounding areas

Embossed   Leather which has been passed through engraved rollers to imprint a pattern on it, usually an imitation of another type of grain, such as pigskin imprinted on to smooth sheepskin

Embossing   Tooling or modelling the grain surface of the leather for decoration

Feather Edge   Very, very fine skiving of edges

Fid   A modelling tool with a curved point

Fourchettes   The finger gussets of gloves

Gloving Kid   High-quality lamb or kid skin with the characteristic of being extremely stretchable

Gold and Silver Kid   Leather from sheep, goat and kid skins which has been treated with leaf or foil metal alloy to give a metallic finish

Grain   The hair side of a skin or hide, sometimes also used to refer to a pattern made by the hair follicles

Hide   Leather made from the skin of a full-grown bovine animal

Hogskin   Grain leather, mainly for gloves, made from pig skin

Kid   Soft leather made from the skin of a young goat

Lamb   Soft leather made from the skin of a young sheep

Lizard   Reptile skins mainly from India and surrounding areas; they sometimes have very beautiful patterns of tiny scales. Can be dyed or left in natural colours

Modelling   Working a design into the surface of the leather while it is damp, using modelling tools to obtain a relief decoration

Morocco   Originally this term applied to goatskin with a natural or hand-produced boarded grain; nowadays it applies to any vegetable-tanned goat skin

Moulding   Wetting the leather and forming into shape with moulds or dyes, then leaving to dry in this shape

Nappa   Soft clothing or gloving leather from unsplit sheep or kid

Parchment   Cleaned and degreased sheepskin which has been dried but not tanned

Paring   Cutting away the thickness of the leather (see *Skiving*)

Patent Leather   Leather which has a flexible, waterproof and highly polished surface produced by repeated coats of varnish and lacquer

Persian   Leather made from the skin of the hair sheep from the Indian sub-continent

Pigskin   Leather produced from the skin of the domestic pig. It has a characteristic pattern made by the hair follicles, which can be seen both on the grain and the flesh sides. The pattern consists of little holes, grouped in threes, all over the skin

Piping   Inserting an extra strip of leather in a seam for a strong edge and a finished appearance (see p43)

Pointing   The small lines of stitches on the back of a glove

Punching   Making holes and patterns with the aid of a punch

Quirk   A small gusset at the base of the finger in some more advanced glove patterns

Rawhide   Cleaned and degreased hide which has been dried but not tanned; it is likely to putrefy if allowed to become damp

Samming   Soaking leather in preparation for moulding, or damping it in preparation for modelling and tooling

Shearling   The skin of a wool sheep with short wool left on for making articles of clothing such as sheepskin jackets

Shoulder   The part of a hide consisting of the neck and shoulder parts of the animal. Often this is good quality leather but has wrinkles and growth marks which can spoil its surface appearance

Skin   Leather from a small animal such as a sheep, goat or deer, as opposed to hide which refers to large bovine animals

Skiver   Very thin grain split for lining, usually from a sheep or goat skin

Skiving   Paring away the thickness of the leather with a special knife in preparation for turning edges or stitching seams (see p33)

Snake   Usually python or watersnake skins are used. Some of these have beautiful patterns and colours but no tensile strength, so they have to be stitched or stuck to other materials before being made up into belts, etc

Split   A layer of leather which has been divided through its thickness to make two or more leathers, often identified as grain split or flesh split

Suede   Leather which has been finished on the flesh side and buffed to a soft nap; mainly used for clothing

Tooling   Ornamenting the surface of leather by hand

Trank   The main hand part of a glove

Turned Edge Work   Articles made from leather which have the edges turned inside and stitched or stuck in position, usually lined (see p41)

Velvet Calf   Calf leather which has been finished on the grain side and buffed to a fine nap

Willow Calf   Usually brown, chrome-tanned calf with a boarded grain. The name was derived from a tanning process using the bark of the willow tree, but this no longer applies